Learn SQL in Three Days

José A. Ramalho

Wordware Publishing, Inc.

Library of Congress Cataloging-in-Publication Data

Ramalho, José A.
    Learn SQL in three days / José A. Ramalho.
      p. cm.
    Includes index.
    ISBN 1-55622-765-5 (pbk.)
    1. SQL (Computer program language).

QA76.73.S67 R392 2000
005.75'6--dc21
                                                  00-049536
                                                          CIP

© 2001, Wordware Publishing, Inc.

All Rights Reserved

2320 Los Rios Boulevard
Plano, Texas 75074

No part of this book may be reproduced in any form or by any means
without permission in writing from Wordware Publishing, Inc.

Printed in the United States of America

ISBN 1-55622-765-5
10 9 8 7 6 5 4 3 2 1
0010

Advantage is a trademark of Extended Systems.

SQLBase is a trademark of Centura Software Corporation.

Other product names mentioned are used for identification purposes only and may be trademarks of their respective companies.

All inquiries for volume purchases of this book should be addressed to Wordware Publishing, Inc., at the above address. Telephone inquiries may be made by calling:

(972) 423-0090

Contents

Introduction ix

Day 1

Chapter 1: Database Overview 3
   Client/Server Architecture 4
   Database Architecture 5
      Desktop Database 5
      Oracle Database 6
      SQL Server 7 6
   Database Objects 7
      Tables 7
      Synonyms 8
      Snapshots 8
      Users 8
      Roles 9
      Indexes 10
      Views 11
      Stored Procedures 11
      Triggers 12
   Summary 12

Chapter 2: SQL Overview 13
   Characteristics of SQL 14
      Procedural Language 14
      Statement Language 15
      Interactive and Embedded SQL 15
   Subdivisions of SQL 16
      DDL (Data Definition Language) 16
      DML (Data Manipulation Language) 16
      DCL (Data Control Language) 16
   Data Types 16
   Database Example 17
   Summary 18

Contents

Chapter 3: SQL Essentials 21
   Types of SQL Declarations 22
      DDL (Data Definition Language) 22
      DML (Data Manipulation Language) 22
   Data Types 23
   The SELECT Command 24
      Examples 25
      Selecting All 26
      Handling Errors 26
      Using SQLTalk. 27
      Selecting Specific Columns 28
      The UNION Operator 28
      The WHERE Clause 29
   The CREATE TABLE Command 30
   The INSERT Command 31
   The DELETE Command 32
   The UPDATE Command 33
   The DROP TABLE Command 34
   Summary 35

Chapter 4: Expressions and Operators 37
   Operators 38
      Precedence of Operators. 40
   The Null Value 40
   Predicates. 40
      Relational Predicates 41
      The BETWEEN Predicate 41
      The NULL Predicate 42
      The EXISTS Predicate 43
      The LIKE Predicate 44
      The IN Predicate. 45
   Summary 45

Chapter 5: Expressions, Columns, and Multiple Tables 47
   Showing Alternate Column Names 48
   Joining Character Fields 49
   Showing Strings of Text Together with the Result 49
   Showing Calculated Columns. 50
   Creating Aliases for Table Names. 51
   Summary 53

Day 2

Chapter 6: Functions 57
   Types of Functions 58
   Aggregate Functions 59
      Using the DISTINCT Clause 62
      Use Restrictions 63
   Summary 64

Chapter 7: Ordering Results 65
   The ORDER BY Clause 66
      Descending Order 67
      Restrictions 68
      Ordering By More Than One Column 68
      Ordering Using Expressions 70
      Ordering Using the Column Header 71
   Summary 71

Chapter 8: Grouping Data 73
   The GROUP BY Clause 74
      Using the WHERE Clause 77
      The Null Value 77
      Using the HAVING Clause 78
      Using the ORDER BY Clause 80
   Summary 81

Chapter 9: Joining Tables 83
   How a Join Works 84
   Creating an Equi-join 87
   Calculations with Columns of Distinct Tables 88
   Joins Based on Non-Equality 90
   Combining the Results with UNION 93
   Summary 95

Chapter 10: Subqueries 97
   Non-Correlated Query 98
   Correlated Query 99
   Values Returned by a Subquery 99
   Restrictions on Subqueries 100
   Using the Aggregate Functions 100
   Using IN and NOT IN 101
   Using EXISTS 103
   Nested Subqueries 105

Using ANY, ALL, and SOME... 109
Summary.. 111

Day 3

Chapter 11: Tables and Indexes..................................... 115
  Tables.. 116
    Data Types... 116
    Constraints.. 117
    Null Values.. 118
    Primary Key.. 118
    Foreign Key.. 119
  The CREATE TABLE Command... 119
    Variations... 121
      Oracle Examples.. 121
      Microsoft SQL Server 7 Examples.......................... 123
    Referential Integrity.. 124
  The DROP TABLE Command... 127
  Indexes... 127
  The CREATE INDEX Command... 129
    The UNIQUE Clause.. 130
  The DROP INDEX Command... 130
  Summary... 131

Chapter 12: Maintaining Tables...................................... 133
  The INSERT Command.. 134
    Inserting Data in Specific Columns........................... 135
    Inserting Data from Other Tables with SELECT................. 137
    Using Expressions.. 139
    Inserting Specific Columns from Other Tables................. 139
  The DELETE Command.. 140
    Deleting Rows from Tables with the Foreign Key............... 141
  The UPDATE Command.. 143
  The ALTER TABLE Command... 144
  Summary... 146

Chapter 13: Views... 147
  Advantages to Using Views... 149
  Creating a View... 149
  Column Names.. 151
  Querying a View... 153
  Deleting a View... 153
  Changing Data with a View... 154

Using the CHECK OPTION Parameter 155
Summary 156

Chapter 14: Embedded SQL. 157
How Embedded SQL Works 158
The Application 158
Behind the Scenes 161
Summary 163

Chapter 15: Miscellaneous 165
Synonyms 166
Users, Privileges, and Roles 168
    Users 168
        Creating a User 168
        Deleting a User 169
    Privileges 170
        Granting Privileges and Roles 173
        Revoking Privileges 174
    Roles 177
        Creating Roles 178
        Granting Roles 178
        Viewing Roles 179
        Deleting Roles 179
Transactions 180
    Atomicity 180
    Consistency 180
    Isolation 180
    Durability 180
    BEGIN TRANSACTION (SQL Server 7) 181
    ROLLBACK 182
    COMMIT 182
Summary 184

Appendix A: Functions 185
Appendix B: Commands 201
Appendix C: Data Types 211
Appendix D: Installing Centura SQLBase 7 219
Appendix E: The Example Database 223
Appendix F: Structure and Contents of Tables 231
Appendix G: Answers to Review Questions 243

Index 251

Introduction

Learn SQL in Three Days is a brief introductory overview to the SQL language ideally suited for introductory programmers who have some experience with relational database software, but no specific experience with SQL. This book provides readers with the basics of the standard SQL language. The information presented here is divided into three parts, as described below.

Day 1

Chapter 1—Database Overview

This chapter introduces the basic concepts of databases. You will learn about the client/server architecture and the main components of a database system such as tables, indexes, views, triggers, and stored procedures. There is also a brief explanation about the differences between the architecture of the Oracle and SQL server databases.

Chapter 2—SQL Overview

This chapter introduces you to the SQL language with a brief explanation about its origin and how it is structured. You will learn the differences between interactive and structured SQL and how the statements of the language are grouped into three main divisions.

Chapter 3—SQL Essentials

This chapter is one of the most important. It gives a complete overview of the language, including the basic statements used by SQL to create, query, and maintain tables in a database. You will learn how to use the SELECT statement, which is the core of the language, to query tables. Other basic statements including INSERT, DELETE, and CREATE TABLE are also shown.

Chapter 4—Expressions and Operators

In order to make full use of the SELECT statement you need to master the operators and expressions of the SQL language to create complex queries.

Introduction

In this chapter you will learn the types of operators and their precedence when different types are evaluated in the same expression. Also, the concepts of the predicate and the most common ones are introduced in this chapter.

Chapter 5—Expressions, Columns, and Multiple Tables

This chapter is a continuation of Chapter 4. It goes deeper into the use of expressions and shows practical examples. You will learn how to create calculated columns, how to create table aliases, and how to mix strings with the query result set.

Day 2

Chapter 6—Functions

Functions are routines used to execute specific calculations or tasks. This chapter shows the types of function used by SQL and how to use them in a query. You will learn about aggregate functions and how they are important for building queries that require summarization or grouping of data in tables.

Chapter 7—Ordering Results

Often when a table is queried, the results are not displayed in an orderly manner. This chapter shows how the SELECT statement's ORDER BY clause can be used to organize the returned table rows in a specific order.

Chapter 8—Grouping Data

Many times we need to group data from several rows in a table in order to get summary results. This is accomplished with the SELECT statement's GROUP BY clause. This chapter covers in full the GROUP BY clause and its specific characteristics. You will also learn how to use this clause with other SELECT clauses.

Chapter 9—Joining Tables

Creating a relationship between two or more tables is the essence of a relational database. This chapter covers all aspects of linking tables using the Join technique. You will learn how to join tables based on equality and non-equality, as well the use of the SELECT statement's UNION clause.

Chapter 10—Subqueries

In order to create complex queries you need to combine two or more queries in a single command. This chapter teaches you how to use subqueries, which are queries that pass their results as predicates to other queries. You will also see the use of aggregated functions and nested queries.

Day 3

Chapter 11—Tables and Indexes

This chapter goes deeper into table creation. It shows details of the CREATE TABLE statement and highlights the differences in the statement between the major database vendors. The concepts of referential integrity, primary keys, and how indexes are created and related to a table are also covered.

Chapter 12—Maintaining Tables

Once created, tables must be maintained and updated. This chapter covers the INSERT, UPDATE, DELETE, and ALTER statements in detail. In addition, you will learn how to delete rows in more than one table using the foreign key features in order to keep referential integrity, as well as how to insert data from other tables directly into the current one.

Chapter 13—Views

This chapter explains the concept of a view, a virtual table that shows data from other tables. The creation, use, and limitations of tables, including situations in which it is better to use a table, are covered.

Chapter 14—Embedded SQL

This chapter demonstrates the concept of embedded SQL with a practical example of how to use the SQL language inside an application. It shows a simple application written in Centura that accesses tables from a demo database.

Chapter 15—Miscellaneous

This chapter addresses several SQL topics, including the creation of synonyms for database objects, granting privileges to users, and transactions. These topics are implemented in a variety of ways by various database vendors, so this chapter shows the general concepts of their use.

Introduction

Appendixes

Appendixes A, B, and C contain an alphabetical summary of the functions, commands, and data types of the SQL language, as well as the Microsoft, Oracle, and Centura variations. The functions and commands that are unique to each database, as well as those that are common to all, are detailed here. Appendix D explains how to install the companion CD, which includes Centura SQLBase. Appendix E shows how to install the example database that comes with the book. Appendix F outlines the contents and structure of the tables in the example database. Appendix G contains the answers to the review questions at the end of each chapter.

The Companion CD

The companion CD-ROM contains an evaluation copy of Centura™ Software Corporation's SQLBase database. This product is a database with characteristics of other major corporate databases and is quite similar to Oracle. The copy distributed with this book is a 60-day trial version that will expire 60 days from the date of installation. After this period you must register the product if you want to continue using it. Installation instructions are included in Appendix D. For more information about SQLBase, check Centura's web site: www.centurasoft.com.

An evaluation copy of Advantage™ Database Server 5.7 from Extended Systems® is also included on the companion CD. This product is a high-performance DBMS for database applications. For more information, see the pages near the end of this book or check www.advantagedatabase.com.

The companion CD also contains an example database and a SQLBase application.

If you have any comments about this book, you may contact the author at jose.antonio@ramalho.com.br.

Day 1

Chapter

1 — Database Overview
2 — SQL Overview
3 — SQL Essentials
4 — Expressions and Operators
5 — Expressions, Columns, and Multiple Tables

Chapter 1
Database Overview

- Client/server architecture
- Database architecture
- Database objects

If you are a developer of corporate databases such as Oracle, Sybase, or DB2, you likely are already familar with the following concepts. However, many developers who work with PC databases or desktop programming languages have little knowledge about the elements that form a real relational database. This chapter focuses on terms and components relating to the main databases.

Client/Server Architecture

In the client/server architecture the database resides in a computer called a server with information shared by several users who run the applications in their local computers, or clients. Such architecture provides better data integrity, because all users are working with the same information. Using business rules, one can enforce controls that are applicable to all users concerning information that is added to the database. The client/server architecture reduces considerably the network traffic, since it returns to the user just the data requested. For example, if a search of a database containing 100,000 records returned just three records, only those three records will be sent to the client machine. In a traditional system, all 100,000 records would be sent through the network. This client/server architecture helps make maintenance tasks such as backing up and restoring much easier because data is located in only one place. Following is the basic structure of this architecture.

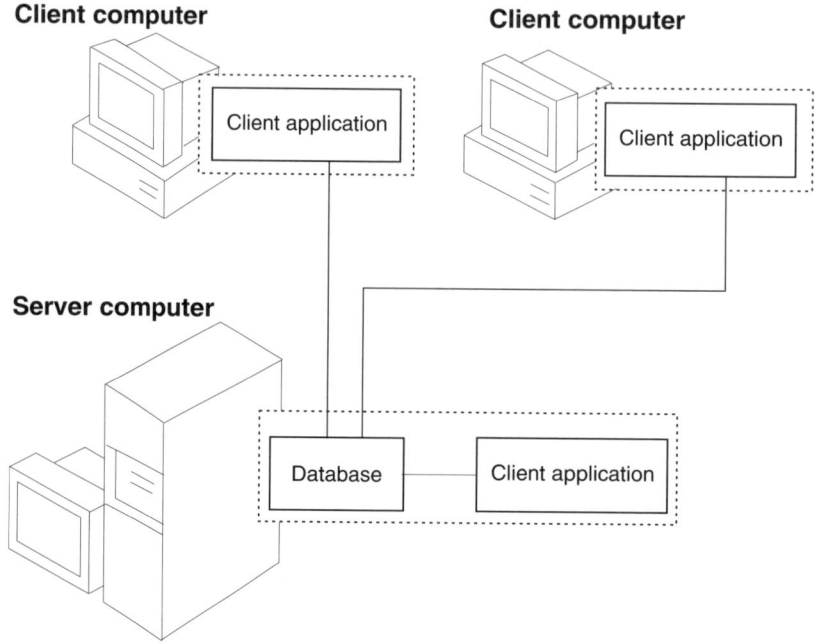

Database Architecture

Desktop Database

If you work with a desktop database such as dBASE, FoxPro, or Clipper, it is important to define the term "database." As an example, a small application to maintain a company's accounts payable could contain the following files:

Invoice.dbf	File with billing data
IndInv01.ntx	Index file to index the bill file by number
IndInv02.ntx	Index file to index the bill file by client
Customer.dbf	File with client data
IndCust01.ntx	Index file to index the file of clients by code
Rel1.frm	File of summary report
Rel2.frm	File of analytical report
Label01.lbl	File of label report
AccREc.exe	Executable program containing the application logic

Generally, all these files are put in a directory to make it easier to control their contents. In this situation, data security is critical, since any one of the files can easily be accidentally deleted. The DBF files normally are called databases by the developer. In the Oracle environment, they are seen as tables that together with other types of files are part of a database.

The developers of Access applications have a view that is closest to the database concept of the corporate databases. To the operating system, an Access database is a file with the extension .MDB. Inside this file the tables, queries, forms, and reports are maintained, along with the application logic (macros and modules).

Physically speaking, databases have different characteristics. In addition, they group information in a particular format according to their architecture.

Oracle Database

Three types of files form the Oracle database. The Datafiles store the logical structures of the database, containing tables and indexes, the Redo Log Files store the changes made in the database that are used in a data recovery process, and the Control Files store the physical structure and the status of the database.

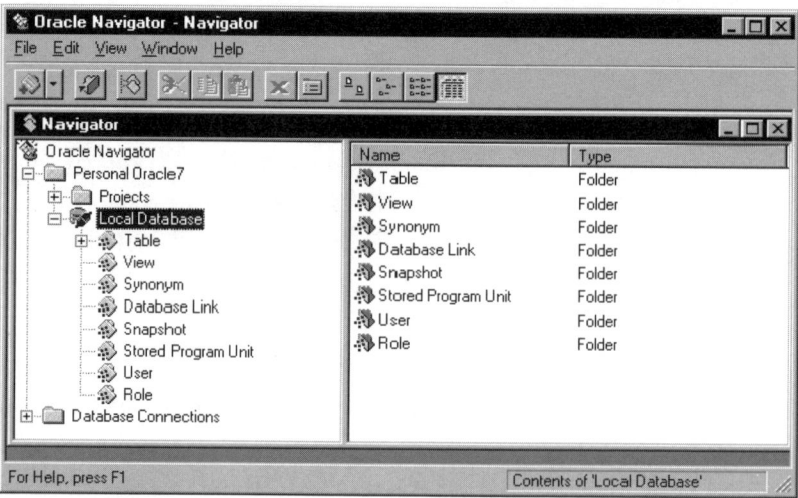

The local database is a concept common to most of the databases. This is the database that is available when the database is loaded.

SQL Server 7

The SQL Server 7 database is divided into several logical components, such as tables, indexes, views, and other elements that are visible to the user. These elements are physically located in two or more files on the disk. The file format and location where the logical elements are written is seamless to the system's user.

A SQL Server 7 server can contain many databases pertaining to several users. A company may have just one database that is used by many employees throughout several departments, or it may have several databases that are exclusively used by specific employees in each department. The following illustration shows the user's view in the form of three tables and their physical implementation through the use of a data file, an index file, and a log file.

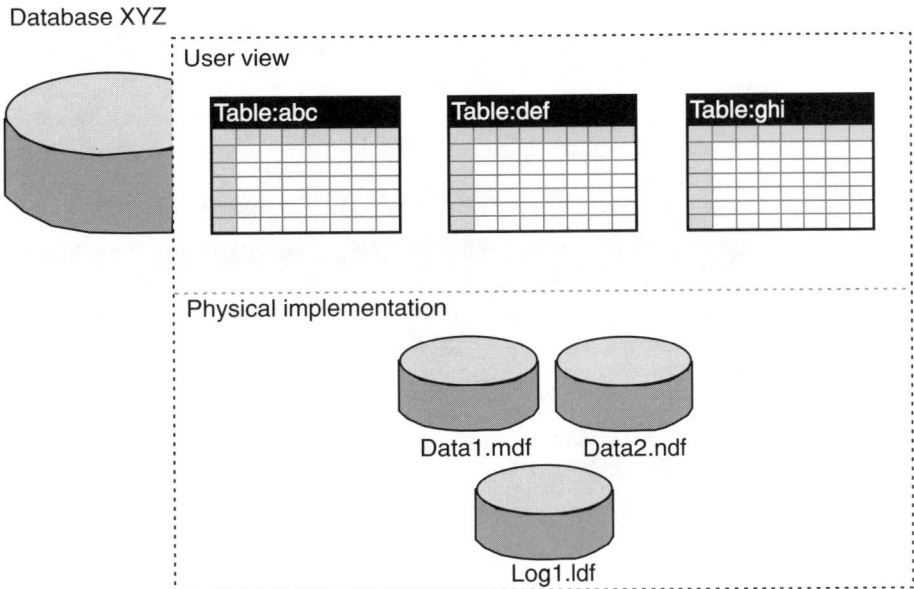

Database Objects

The components defined and stored in a database as tables, views, indexes, synonyms, database links, roles, snapshots, users, triggers, packages, stored procedures, and functions are all database objects. This section discusses the objects that are common to most databases.

Tables

Tables are the heart of a database. They store data grouped in the form of rows and columns. The columns correspond to the table fields. The rows are the records. In a database environment such as Oracle the term "table" is the default to refer to what in a PC database is called a "data file." For example, a sales system may contain several tables: one to store client data (customer), a second to store order data, another for code and description of products, etc.

8 ■ Chapter 1

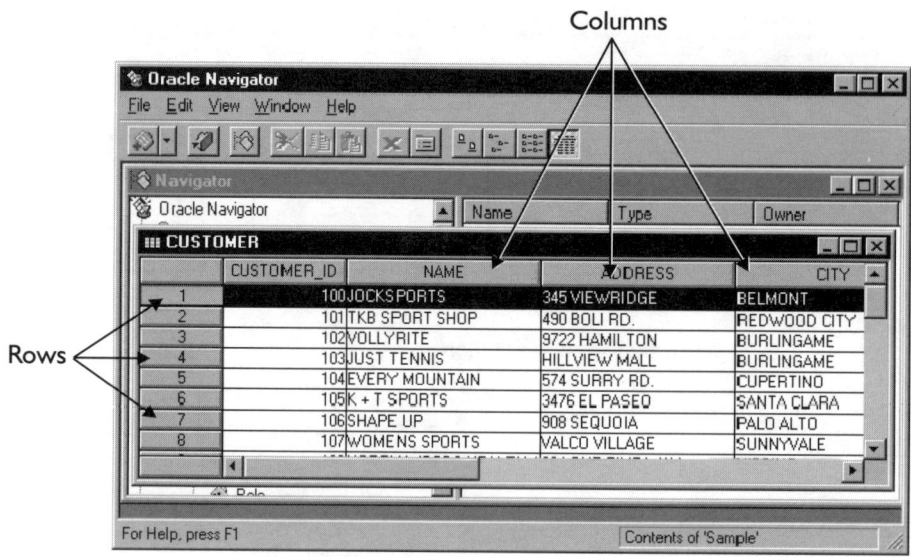

Synonyms

A *synonym* is an alias for a table, view, or program unit. Synonyms are used in those situations where you want to hide the real location of a table and its owner, or to make accessing an object easier through the use of a simpler name.

Snapshots

A *snapshot* is a copy of the entire table or part of a table. It reflects the current status of the table that is being copied. The source table is known as the master table. There are two types of snapshots: Read-Only, also known as publish-and-subscribe publication, and Updatable, also known as update-anywhere replication. The Read-Only snapshot does not allow changes, while the Updatable snapshot allows changes in the local copy and periodically updates the master table.

Users

Anyone who accesses a database is a *user*, and each user has a name and a password. During the installation of a database, users and passwords are created and used to access the database the first time. The database administrator is in charge of creating the users and passwords. The following figure shows the users created during the installation of Oracle.

Database Overview ■ 9

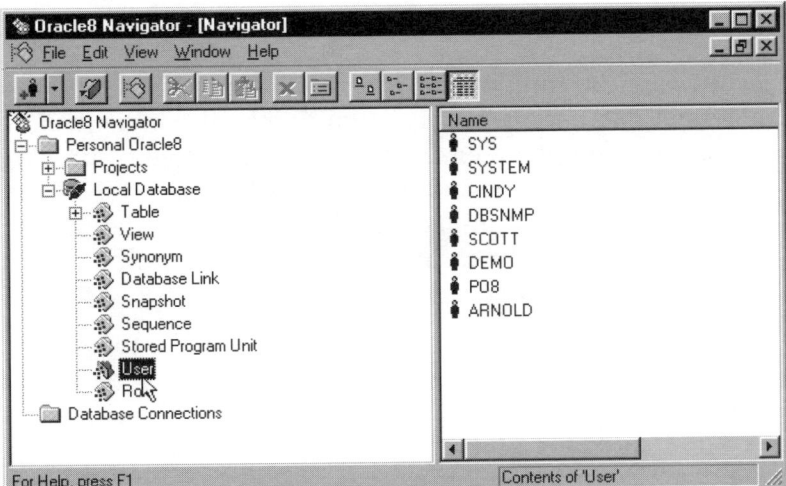

To change a user's password, just click on the user name. In the dialog box that appears, enter the new password.

Roles

A *role* is a method of granting privileges to work with a database. The person who creates a database object can grant privileges to either a user or a role. When a role is attributed to a user, he or she obtains all the privileges associated to that role.

In the figure below, user Scott has two roles attributed to him: CONNECT and RESOURCE.

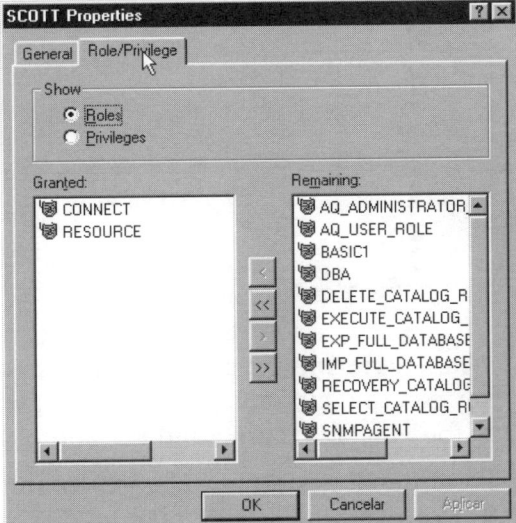

Indexes

Indexes are the components of a database that are used to speed up data access. A database index is similar to a book's index, where instead of skimming through an entire book to find a page containing specific information, you simply use the index to locate the subject and its corresponding page number. Without an index, the search for a certain record takes more time, since the records are stored by order of creation, rather than in any logical order.

Once the index is created, all the changes made to a table are automatically reflected in the index. A database index can be associated to a specific column or a combination of several columns, and several indexes can be created for a table. Some indexes are automatically created, as is the case with primary key columns.

In the Employees table shown below, the index is based on the emp_id column.

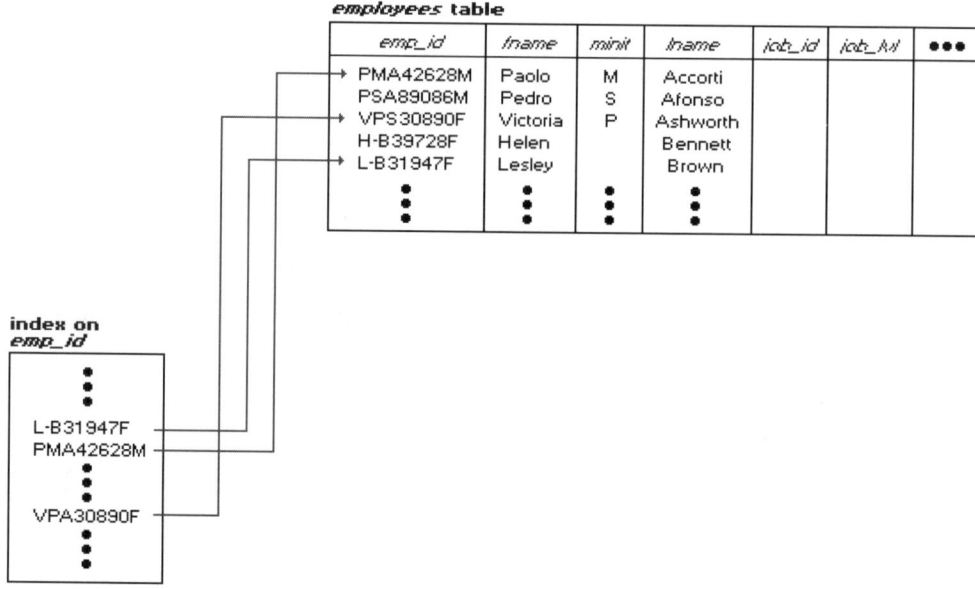

When performing a search in the Employees table, the server detects the key column and searches the index, which contains a copy of the contents of the emp_id column and the address of its row inside the table.

For optimal performance, each column should have an index associated to it. However, indexes do take up disk space, and often they are never used.

Views

A *view* is a virtual table with its contents defined by a database query. The view is not a physical table, but a set of instructions that returns a set of data. The figure below shows two tables that serve as the basis for the creation of a query.

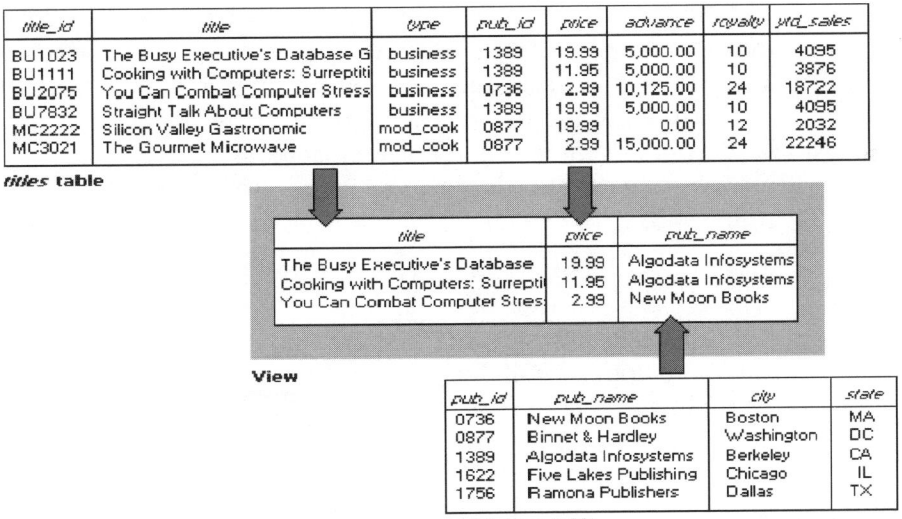

Stored Procedures

The data in a database can be accessed only through the execution of Transact-SQL commands. When creating an application to serve as the interface with the database, the developer can choose to create a SQL program that is locally stored and sent to the server to be executed there, or to create and maintain the program in the server itself in stored procedures that can be triggered by a program in the client machine. A *stored procedure* can accept parameters (values that are passed to a procedure) to be processed. However, unlike functions, they do not return any value. Once a stored procedure is created, it can be used by any application that accesses the database. Stored procedures are created with the Transact-SQL CREATE PROCEDURE command and are changed by the ALTER PROCEDURE command.

Triggers

A *trigger* is a stored procedure that is automatically executed when a SQL INSERT, UPDATE, or DELETE command changes data in a table. One of its most common uses is to force limitations that are more complex than those allowed by the CHECK constraint, which limits the type of information inserted in a column. A trigger can be associated with the INSERT command, which makes a query to other tables and returns a logic value that limits data attributed to certain columns. For example, you can create a trigger to run an instant replication. In other words, when a row is inserted in database Z, a row with the same information is added to database Y. In addition, when a row is deleted from a table, the trigger deletes rows in other tables that are associated to it. A trigger is treated as a transaction and can be rolled back when a problem is detected.

All of these database objects are created through standard SQL commands or in the dialect used by a particular database. Many products have graphical interfaces and wizards that create and maintain objects without having to code a SQL declaration. Even so, it is important to know how each declaration is related to the creation and maintenance of the object functions.

Summary

This chapter provided an overview of database components. The next chapter is an overview of the SQL language.

Review Questions

1. Where does the database in a client/server architecture reside?
2. What is a table?
3. What is an index?
4. What is a view?
5. What is a role?
6. What is a stored procedure?
7. What is a trigger?

Chapter 2
SQL Overview

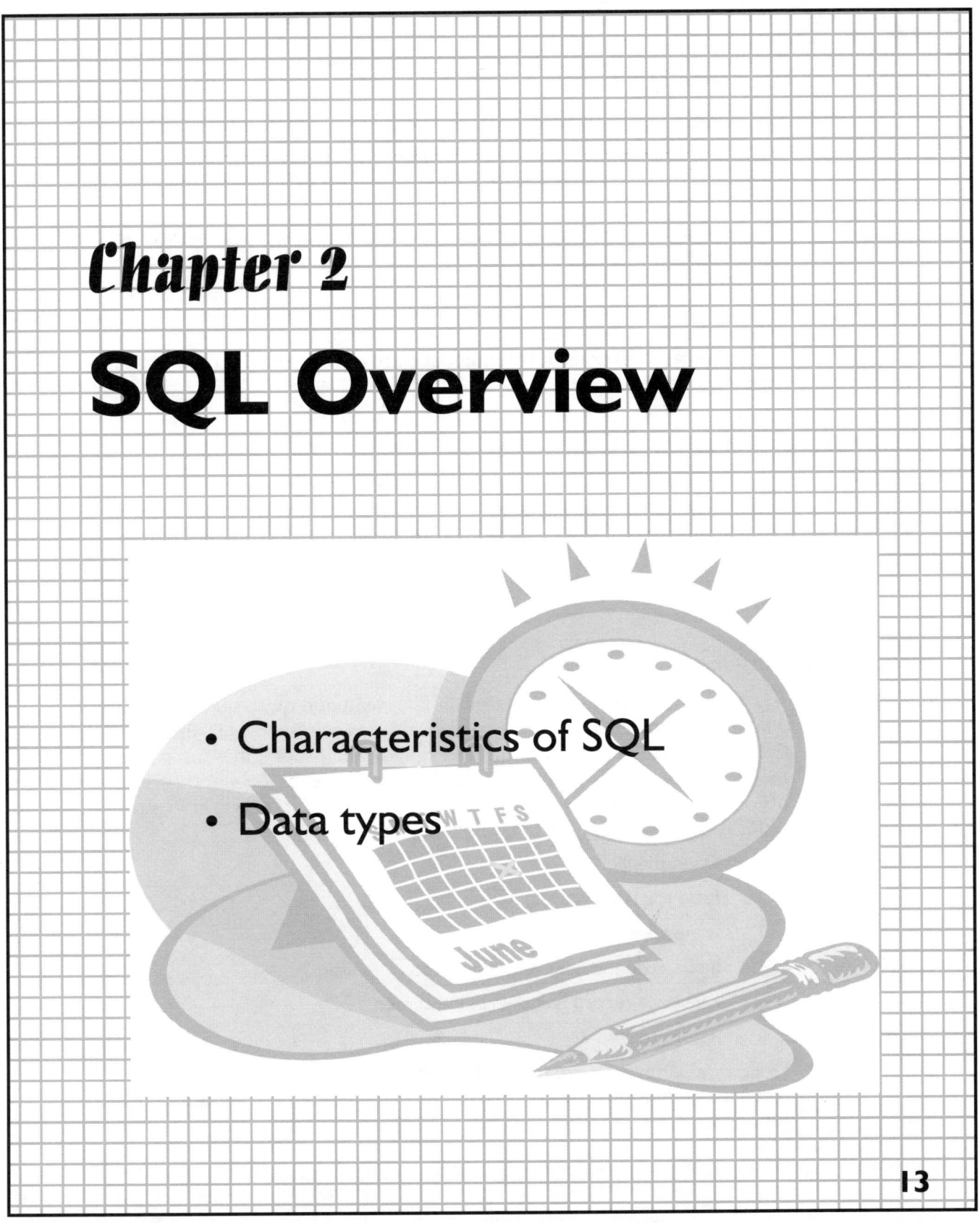

- Characteristics of SQL
- Data types

SQL, structured query language, was developed at IBM. It was created to define, change, and query data contained in a relational database. IBM researcher E.F. Codd first proposed the relational database model approximately 30 years ago.

The language's simplicity allowed it to become a standard for accessing databases and was gradually incorporated by major database vendors. Like any other language, it has been updated over time and has incorporated new resources as databases have evolved. Inevitably, database vendors have created their own extensions to the language. Among the most popular variations of this language are Sybase and Microsoft's Transact-SQL, Oracle's PL/SQL, and IBM's DB2.

Characteristics of SQL

A committee was created to standardize SQL in an attempt to make it platform independent. The SQL standard is defined by the ANSI (American National Standards Institute). Learning basic ANSI-standard SQL is the first step for a programmer, regardless of the SQL dialect he or she uses. The following sections describe some of the characteristics of the SQL language.

Procedural Language

It is not difficult to learn SQL, since it is a clean and quite specialized language. SQL, however, is not a procedural language, such as C, BASIC, Cobol, or Pascal. With procedural languages, the programmer must tell the computer what to do step by step. For example, if you want to view a list of records in a client file in which the state is TX, a program in a procedural language requires the following steps:

1. Open the file.
2. Read the first record.
3. Is the state field TX?
4. If not, read the next record and return to step 3.
5. If yes, the record is shown in the screen.
6. Return to step 3.

Procedural languages are normally quicker to execute; however, they require a greater effort when there is any change in the structure of data contents.

Statement Language

With a statement language, you tell the computer what you want and it fulfills your request. Performing the previous query in a statement language such as SQL requires the user to request the following:

1. Show all records in which the state is TX.

Statement languages, although less powerful in terms of formatting the result, are quite flexible and adequate for queries made to a relational database.

Interactive and Embedded SQL

The SQL language can be used in two ways: interactively or embedded inside another program.

The SQL language is used interactively to directly operate a database and produce the desired results. The user enters a SQL command that is immediately executed. Most databases have a tool that allows the interactive execution of the SQL language. These include SQLBase's SQLTalk, Oracle's SQL Plus, and Microsoft's SQL Server 7 Query Analyzer.

The second way to execute a SQL command is by embedding it in another language such as Cobol, Pascal, BASIC, C, or Visual Basic. The result of the embedded SQL command is passed to the variables in the host program, which in turn will deal with them. (See Chapter 14 for a more thorough discussion of embedded SQL.)

The figure on the following page shows the interactive execution of a SQL command.

The combination of SQL with a fourth-generation language brings together the best of two worlds, and allows the creation of user interfaces and database access in one application.

Chapter 2

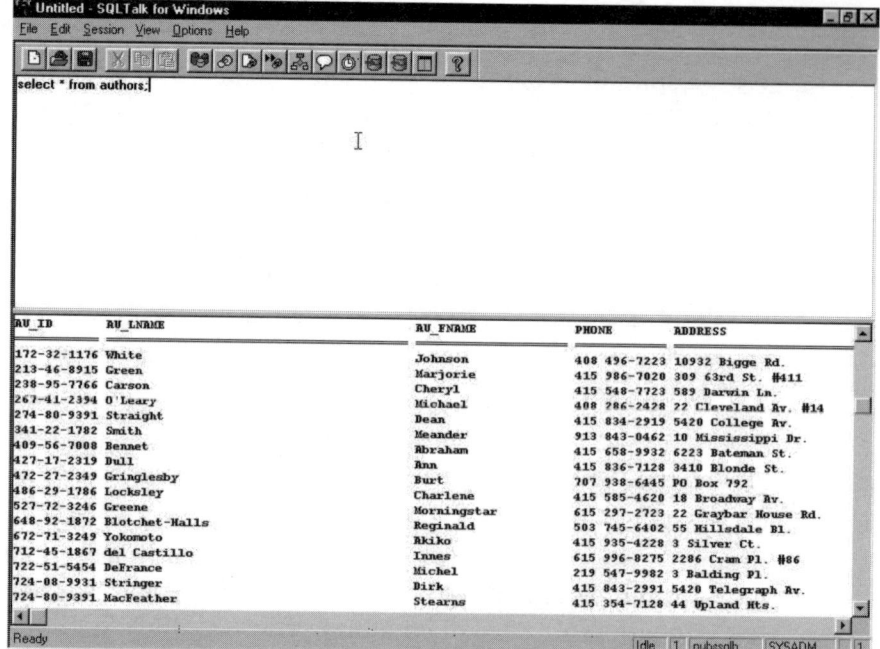

Subdivisions of SQL

Regardless of whether SQL is embedded or used interactively, it can be divided into three groups of commands, depending on their purpose. Each of these types of commands is discussed in later chapters.

DDL (Data Definition Language)

Data definition language is the part of SQL that is responsible for the creation of objects such as tables, indexes, and views. These commands include:

CREATE TABLE
CREATE VIEW
CREATE INDEX

DML (Data Manipulation Language)

Data manipulation language includes those commands that run queries and changes in data. It includes the following:

SELECT
UPDATE
DELETE

DCL (Data Control Language)

The commands that form data control language are related to the security of the database, performing tasks of assigning privileges so users can access certain objects in the database. These are the DCL commands:

GRANT
REVOKE

Data Types

When creating a database table, you must define the data type for each field. SQL has some standard data types, but the many dialects of SQL have introduced their own variations to extend the language, such as the inclusion of fields to store objects as images, movies, scalar vectors, etc. The most common types of data that are stored in a table are text, number, and date. The definition and terminology of data types is one area where there are great differences between standard SQL and its dialects. The SQL standard recognizes just the text and numeric data types. The chart below defines the basic types:

Table 2-1. Data Types

Text	
Char or Character	String of characters that must be inside quotation marks.
Numeric	
Dec or Decimal	Decimal number defined by two parts: precision and scale. Precision indicates the number of significant digits. Scale indicates how many decimal places the number has.
Numeric	Identical to dec, but the maximum number of digits cannot exceed the specified precision.
Int	Number without the decimal part.
Smallint	Identical to int, but with a size limit.
Float	Floating-point number with exponential base 10.

Table 2-1. Data Types (continued)

Real	Identical to float, except that an argument is not used to specify the size.
Double or Double Precision	Identical to real, but with greater precision.

Database Example

The best way to learn a programming language is to practice the concepts you learn. This book was written using a database that simulates a publishing house and bookstore. The structure of this database and the relationships of its tables are shown below. Appendix F shows the contents of each table in the database.

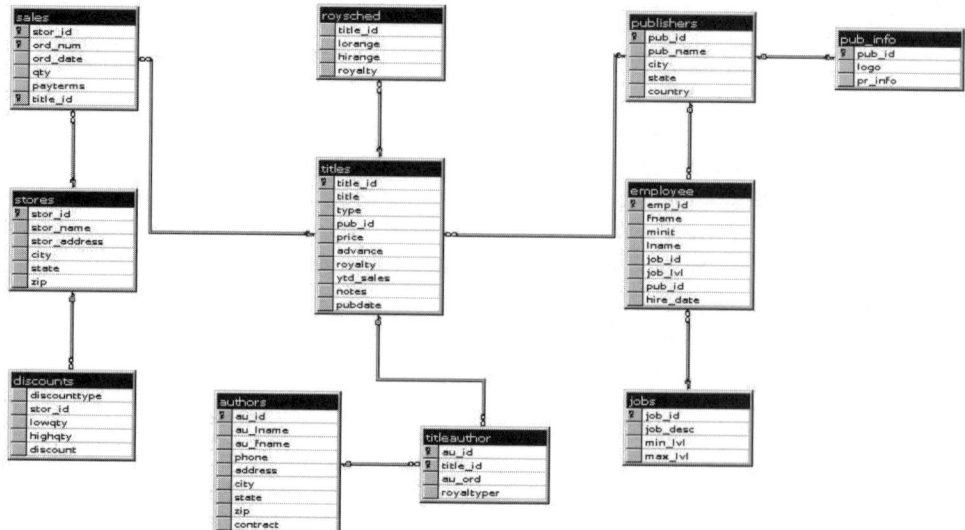

Summary

This chapter gave an overview of the structured query language, the standard database language. The next chapter introduces essential concepts of SQL, including the SELECT command.

Review Questions

1. What is the difference between interactive SQL and embedded SQL?
2. What are the different groups of SQL commands?
3. What is the purpose of DDL commands?
4. What is the purpose of DML commands?
5. What is the purpose of DCL commands?
6. What are data types?
7. What is the difference between int and float types?

Chapter 3
SQL Essentials

- The SELECT command
- The CREATE TABLE command
- The INSERT command
- The DELETE command
- The UPDATE command

With just a dozen commands and functions, a developer is able to perform most activities related to querying and manipulating a database. In this chapter you will learn how to create queries to an existing database, how to create a table, and how to insert and delete data.

These are the commands and functions discussed in this chapter:

Commands	Functions
SELECT	SUM( )
INSERT	AVG( )
DELETE	MAX( )
UPDATE	MIN( )
CREATE TABLE	COUNT( )
	SYSDATE( )

Types of SQL Declarations

Let us review the types of declarations. The SQL declarations, or commands, are divided into two main categories: DDL and DML, depending on their function. (See the previous chapter for an explanation of the data control language.)

DDL (Data Definition Language)

DDL, or data definition language, is the part of SQL used to define the data and objects in a database. When these commands are used, entries are made in a data dictionary in the SQL server. Following are some DDL commands:

Command	Explanation
CREATE TABLE	Creates a table
CREATE INDEX	Creates an index
ALTER TABLE	Changes or inserts a column in a table
DROP TABLE	Eliminates the table from the database
DROP INDEX	Eliminates an index

DML (Data Manipulation Language)

DML, the language for manipulating data, is the part of SQL used to recover or manipulate data. Its commands are responsible for the queries and changes made to tables. These are some of the most important commands in this category:

Day 1

Command	Explanation
SELECT	This is the main command of the language; it is used to recover data from a table or view
INSERT	Inserts a row in a table
DELETE	Deletes a row in a table
UPDATE	Changes the contents of the columns (fields) in the table
COMMIT	Writes the changes to disk
ROLLBACK	Undoes the changes made after the last commit

Data Types

Before continuing with the commands, you need to know the data types that can be stored in the database you are using. See Appendix C for a detailed description of the data types permitted in specific databases. To create a table, you must provide information such as the table's name, and the name and data type that will be stored in each field. Table 3-1 lists the data types for SQLBase:

Table 3-1. Data Types

Data Type	Description
Char	Character data type with fixed size of up to 254 characters.
Date	Stores only the date.
Datetime or Timestamp	When part of the input argument is omitted, SQLBase assumes the default 0, which converts the date to 30/12/1899 and 12:00 a.m.
Decimal or Dec	Supports up to 15 digits (−999999999999999 to +999999999999999). If nothing is specified, the precision 5 and scale 0 are assumed.
Double precision	Numeric data type of floating-point and double precision.
Float	When the precision is between 1 and 21, the data type will have simple precision. Between 22 and 53, the precision is double.
Integer or Int	An integer data type with precision of up to 10 digits (−2,147,483,648 up to +2,147,483,647).
Long Varchar	Stores characters or binary objects. This is equivalent to the data type blob.

Table 3-1. Data Types (continued)

Data Type	Description
Number	This is a super set from other data types. It supports precision of up to 22 digits.
Real	Numeric data type of floating-point and simple precision.
Smallint	This data type has no fractional digits. The digits to the right of the decimal point are truncated. You can have precision of up to five digits (from −32,768 to +32,767).
Time	Stores only the hour.
Varchar	Character data type with fixed size of up to 254 characters.

The SELECT Command

This command is the essence of the SQL language, and we will discuss it throughout this book. Its purpose is to find, recover, and show data that answers the user's query. It specifies the following information:

- The tables or views to be searched for in the database
- The search conditions
- The sequence in which data are shown

Basic syntax:

```
SELECT [*] [ALL | DISTINCT]
[name =] expression
[expression [AS name]]
FROM <table_name> [correlation_name] <view_name>
WHERE <search_condition>
[GROUP BY <integer_constant>] <column_name>]
[HAVING <search_condition>]
[ORDER BY <integer_constant> [ASC] [DESC]] <column_name>]
```

Arguments:

*	Selects all the columns in a table.
ALL	The default in a SELECT command is to recover all the rows.
DISTINCT	Does not show duplicated rows.
expression	A selection list of expressions separated by commas. An expression can be a column name, a constant, a checked variable, the result of a function, or a system keyword.

FROM
: Contains the names of the tables or views resulting in a set of rows.

correlation_name
: A related name can be used to designate a preceding table or view.

WHERE <search_condition>
: Specifies a search condition for the basic tables or views. The search condition cannot contain aggregate functions.

GROUP BY <integer_constant/column_name>
: This clause groups the resulting rows of a query, according to the column names. When the column by which the grouping occurs is an expression with more than one column, you must specify the number that indicates its relative position in the selection list.

HAVING <search_condition>
: This clause allows you to establish a search condition with a group of rows resulting from a GROUP BY clause or by grouped columns.

ORDER BY <integer_constant/column_name>
: Specifies the order of rows in a result table. The rows can be ordered by more than one column. When the order column is derived from a function or arithmetic expression, the column must be specified by an integer that indicates the relative number of its position in the SELECT command. Optionally, ASC or DESC, indicating the ascending or descending order, can follow each column name or number.

Examples

To run a query using the SELECT command, you must know the structure of the tables that will be queried. You also need to know at least the name of the columns you want to recover or process in some way. Initially we will work with the Authors table, which has the following structure:

Name	Data Type	Length	Description
AU_ID	VARCHAR	11	Author ID
AU_LNAME	VARCHAR	40	Last name
AU_FNAME	VARCHAR	20	First name
PHONE	CHAR	12	Telephone
ADDRESS	VARCHAR	40	Address
CITY	VARCHAR	20	City
STATE	CHAR	2	State
ZIP	CHAR	5	ZIP Code

The SELECT command requires that you specify which columns of a table you want to show and which table contains those fields:

```
SELECT column(s)_name  FROM table_name
```

The name or address of a table must follow the word FROM where two columns are specified.

Selecting All

To select all the columns in a table, you can use the asterisk symbol (*) in place of all the column names. Therefore, to show all the rows and columns in a table, use the following syntax:

```
SELECT * FROM table_name
```

Handling Errors

When using programs that allow the interactive use of the SQL language, you likely will run into some typing or syntax errors. When this occurs, the program shows an error message, which varies from one program to another. Below is an example of an error returned by SQLTalk.

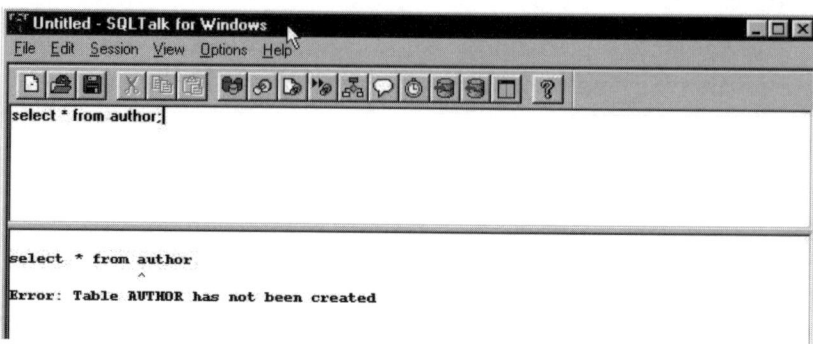

Other programs show different messages for the same error, such as this one generated in SQL Server 7.

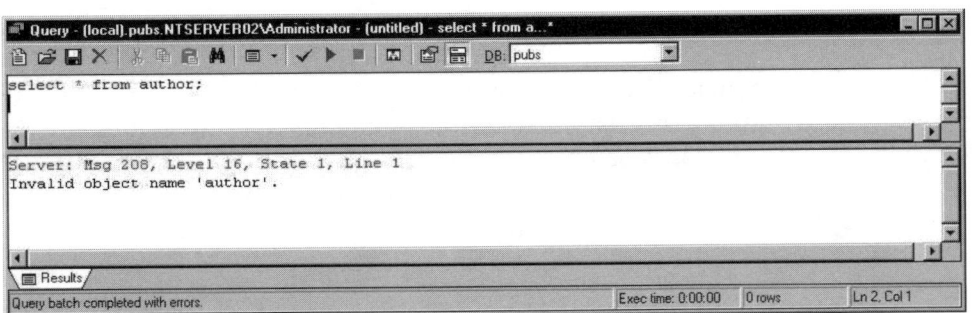

If you find these types of errors, simply correct them and run the command again.

Most programs require a semicolon at the end of the command line.

Using SQLTalk

If you decide to follow along with the examples using the SQLTalk program of the SQLBase database that comes with the book, see Appendix D for installation instructions. Below is the result of the SELECT * FROM authors command in this program.

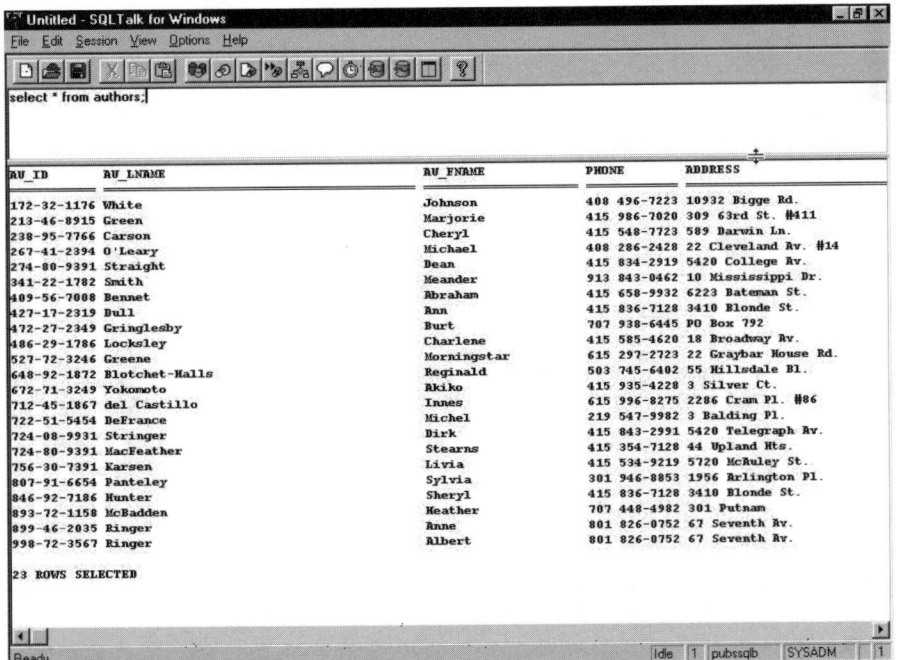

When there are more rows than can appear in the window, use the scroll bars to move the text.

Selecting Specific Columns

Instead of showing all the columns, you can request a list of specific columns. This list must contain the names of the columns separated by commas. The order of the columns is not important. The code below selects the columns containing the first name, last name, and telephone number of each author.

```
SELECT au_fname, au_lname, phone FROM authors;
```

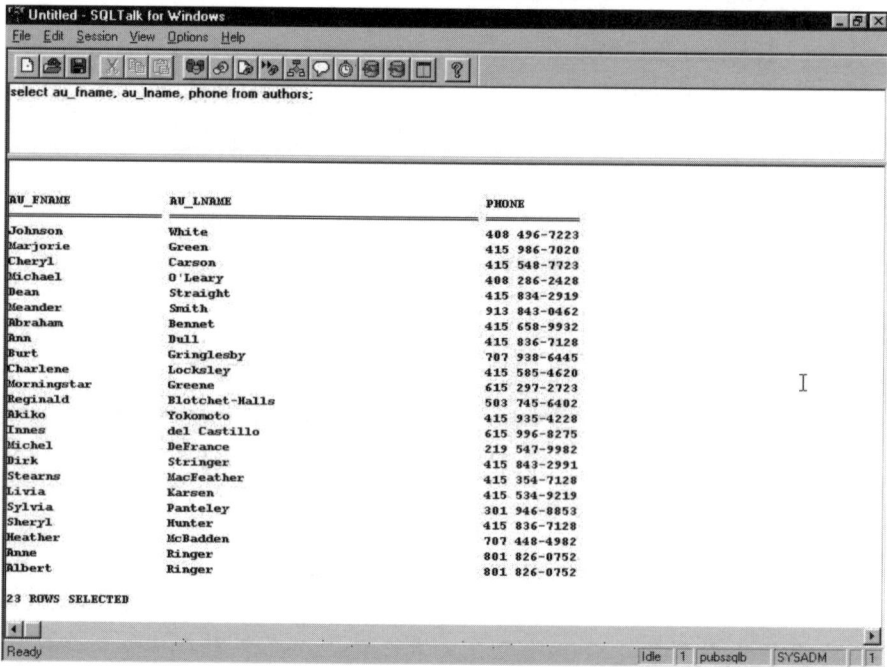

The UNION Operator

The UNION operator can be used between SELECT statements to combine the results of two or more queries into a single result set consisting of all the rows belonging to all queries in the union. Duplicated rows are eliminated by default.

```
SELECT
UNION [ALL]
SELECT
[ORDER BY <integer_constant> [ASC] [DESC]]
```

ALL When this clause is specified, duplicated rows are not eliminated.

ORDER BY This clause orders a set of rows of the final result that come from the union of two or more tables.

The WHERE Clause

The WHERE clause allows you to filter the query in order to limit the number of rows returned. When you execute the following command:

SELECT au_lname, au_fname, state FROM authors;

three columns for each of 23 records are returned. By adding the WHERE clause, we can indicate that we want to view just those rows in which the contents of a certain field fulfill a specific condition. For example, let's say we want to list the fields just for those authors who do not live in California. To do that, we use the comparison operator "<>" (explained in Chapter 4) and specify the contents of the field inside single quotes. The search is case sensitive, so when 'ca' is specified instead of 'CA,' the result will be different.

SELECT au_lname, au_fname, state FROM authors WHERE state <>'CA';

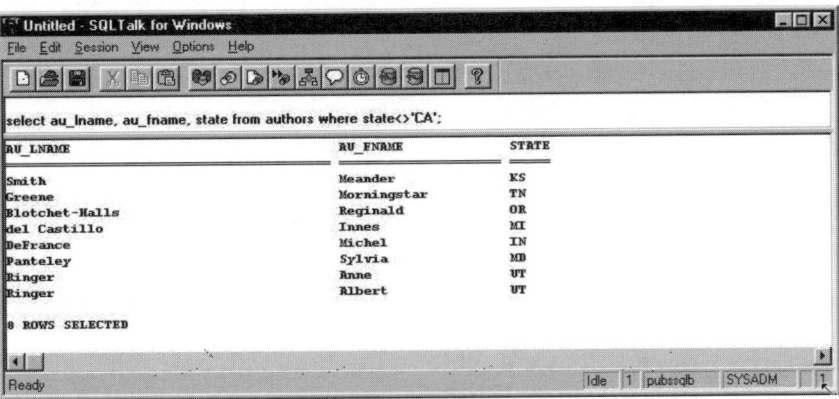

Note that only eight rows were returned. The WHERE clause is quite powerful when combined with logical operators that allow the use of multiple restrictions. For example, try listing all the authors who do not live in California and do not have a contract signed (Contract field=0).

In this case we use the operator AND (logical AND):

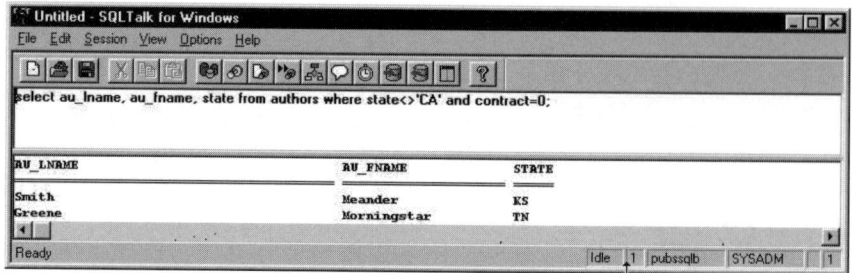

Only two records are returned.

The CREATE TABLE Command

The purpose of the CREATE TABLE command is to create a new table in the database. The number of tables in each database and the number of columns per table depend on the database you are using. For example, the SQL Server 7 database allows up to two billion tables per database, and up to 1,024 columns per table. The number of rows per table is limited only by the available physical space. The maximum size of bytes per row is 8,092.

A table is created in the current database, unless another database is specified. Here is the basic syntax of the CREATE TABLE command:

```
CREATE TABLE <table_name>
( <column_name> <data_type> [<size>],
  <column_name> <data_type> [<size>],...);
```

table_name	This is the name of the table to be created.
column_name	This specifies the name of the column in the table.
<data_type>	Specifies the column data type.
<size>	Specifies the size of the column (optional).

Next we will create a table in the Pubssqlb example database. This table will be called Demo1 and will contain three columns: code with type int, name with type char and size 20, and state with type char and size 2. To make the code easier to read, each column definition is on a different line.

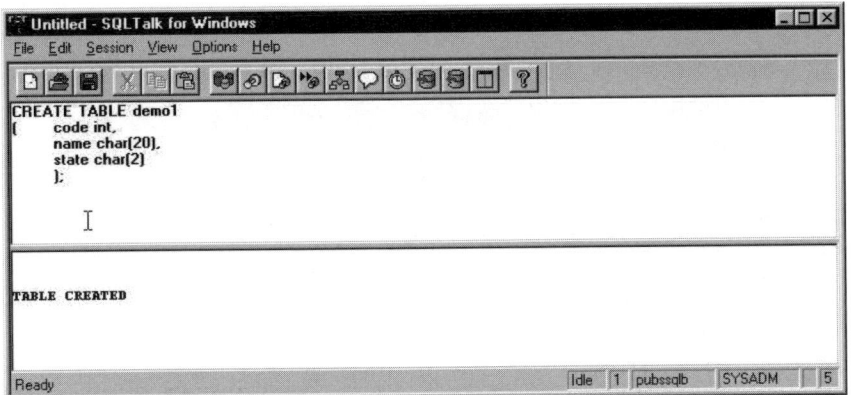

If you try to execute the command again, i.e., to create a table with a name identical to an existing table, the program will show an error message.

The INSERT Command

This command inserts a new row in the table, filling the columns with specific values. It is not necessary to assign contents to all fields.

Basic syntax:

```
INSERT [INTO] {<table_sources>} { } [(column_list)] VALUES
({DEFAULT | constant_expression }[,...n]     )
```

Arguments:

INTO	Indicates the name of the table that will receive data.
column_list	A list of the columns that will receive data. They must appear inside parentheses and are separated by commas. If the values specified by VALUES are not in the same order as the columns, the column_list option must be used to specify which columns will receive those values.
VALUES	Specifies the list of values that will be inserted.
DEFAULT	Attributes the default value to the column. When a default value is not defined, it attributes null.
constant_expression	This is a literal value, expression, or variable.

Examine the next example. First we create a table called Demo2. Then we insert four records in the table. Note that the third record that was inserted has only two fields with contents. For this reason, it was necessary to specify the name of the fields to receive the specified values.

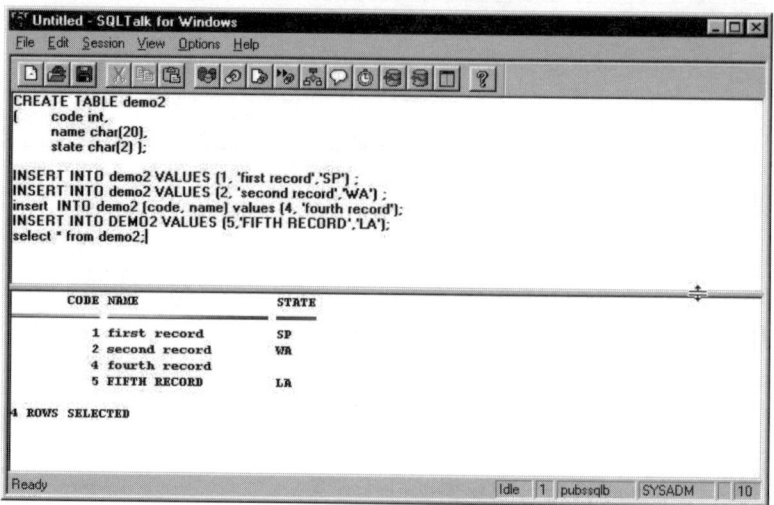

 **Note** Although the basic syntax of a SQL declaration is the same, different databases interpret the same declaration differently. Some require a certain clause while others consider it optional. Microsoft's SQL Server 7 allows the use of the INTO clause with the INSERT command. Oracle and SQLBase require the INTO clause. The contents of the fields must be specified inside double quotation marks in SQLBase, while in SQL Server 7 it can be done with single quotes. These little differences can make life difficult for programmers who switch from one database to another.

The DELETE Command

The DELETE command removes from a table or view those rows that fulfill some specified condition.

Basic syntax:

```
DELETE FROM table_name WHERE condition
```

For example, to delete a row with a state field of SP from the Demo2 table, use the following command:

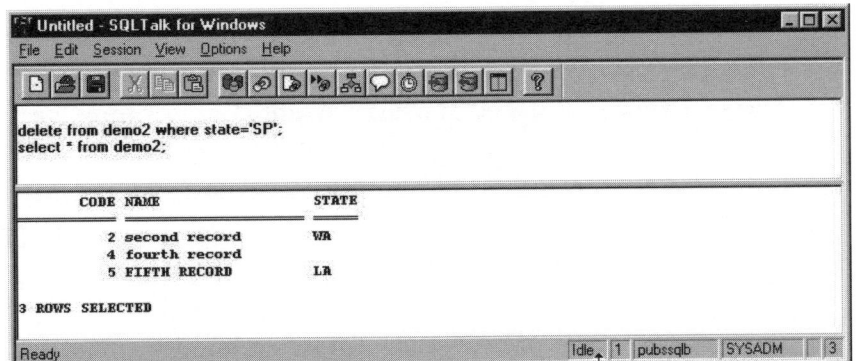

The UPDATE Command

This command allows you to update one or more fields in a row or group of rows of a table or view. The contents of each field must be adjusted with the SET clause. When more than one column is updated, the column=value pairs must be separated by commas. Identity columns cannot be updated.

Basic syntax:

```
UPDATE table
  SET column=value
  WHERE condition

UPDATE {<table_or_view>} SET {column_name =
{expression | DEFAULT} |
@variable = expression} [,...n] [FROM {<table_or_view> |
(select_statement) [AS] table_alias
[ (column_alias [,...m]) ] | <table_or_view> CROSS JOIN <table_or_view> |
INNER [<join_hints>] JOIN <table_or_view> ON <join_condition> |
 <rowset_function> }[, ...n] ] [WHERE <search_conditions> |
CURRENT OF {} [GLOBAL] cursor_name } | cursor_variable_name}} ]
[OPTION (<query_hints>, [,...n] )]
```

Arguments:

SET   Specifies a list of columns to be updated.

column_name

           The name of the column to be updated. If it refers to a table other than the current one, it must be preceded by the name of the table/database.

expression	The new contents of the column; can be the result of a subselect that returns only one value.
DEFAULT	Indicates that the current contents must be replaced with the default value previously defined when the table was created.
FROM	Specifies that another table will be used to provide the updating criteria of the operation.
WHERE	Specifies the conditions that must be met to limit the number of rows that will be updated.

In the next example, the contents of the Comments field of all the rows is changed to "n/a":

```
UPDATE demo1a
SET comments ="n/a"
```

In the next example we use the WHERE clause to filter the changes. We will change the contents of the State field of the record in which the Code field is 4. This record did not have the contents of the State field attributed when the row was inserted.

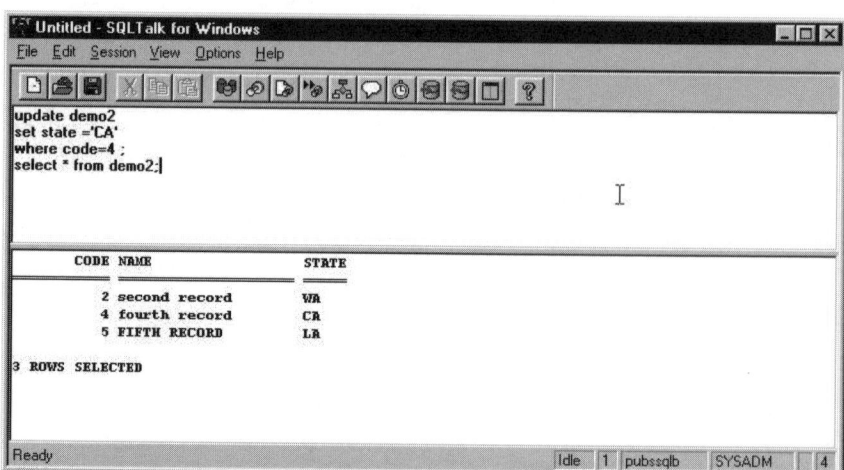

The DROP TABLE Command

Use the DROP TABLE command to remove a table from the database.

This command physically removes the table from the database, thus eliminating its structure and data.

Basic syntax:

```
DROP TABLE table_name
```

The next example removes the Demo1 table from the current database:

```
DROP TABLE demo1
```

In the example below, the command is executed twice. The first time it is executed, the Demo1 table is deleted. The second time an error message is issued, since the Demo1 table does not exist in the database.

To remove a table that is in another database you need to specify the scheme or complete path of the table.

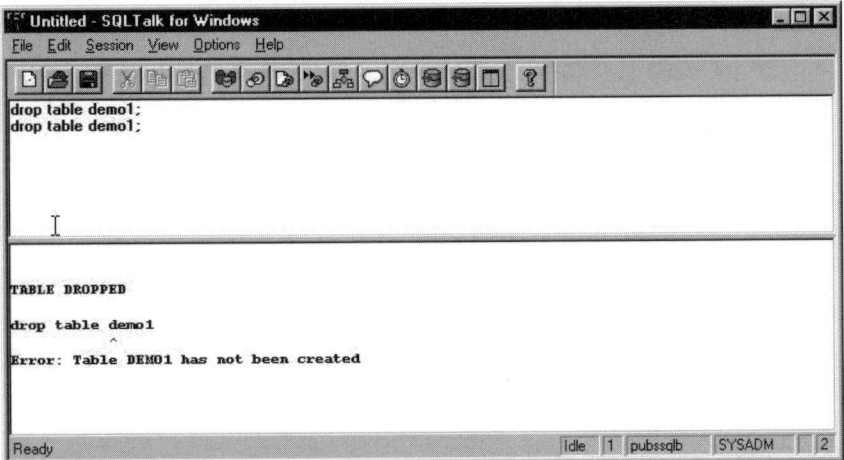

Summary

This chapter gave you a brief introduction to the SQL language and its most important commands. With this basic information, you can query, navigate, and even create tables in many databases. Expressions and operators, which are used within the commands, are explained in the next chapter.

Review Questions

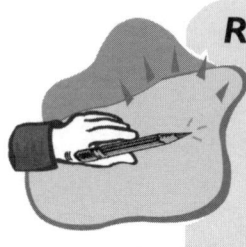

1. What is the purpose of the SELECT command?
2. Write the syntax of the SELECT command.
3. What is the purpose of the asterisk (*) in syntax?
4. What is the purpose of the ALL clause?
5. What is the purpose of the WHERE clause?
6. What is the purpose of the CREATE TABLE command?
7. What is the purpose of the INSERT command?
8. What is the purpose of the DELETE command?
9. What is the purpose of the UPDATE command?
10. What is the purpose of the DROP TABLE command?

Chapter 4
Expressions and Operators

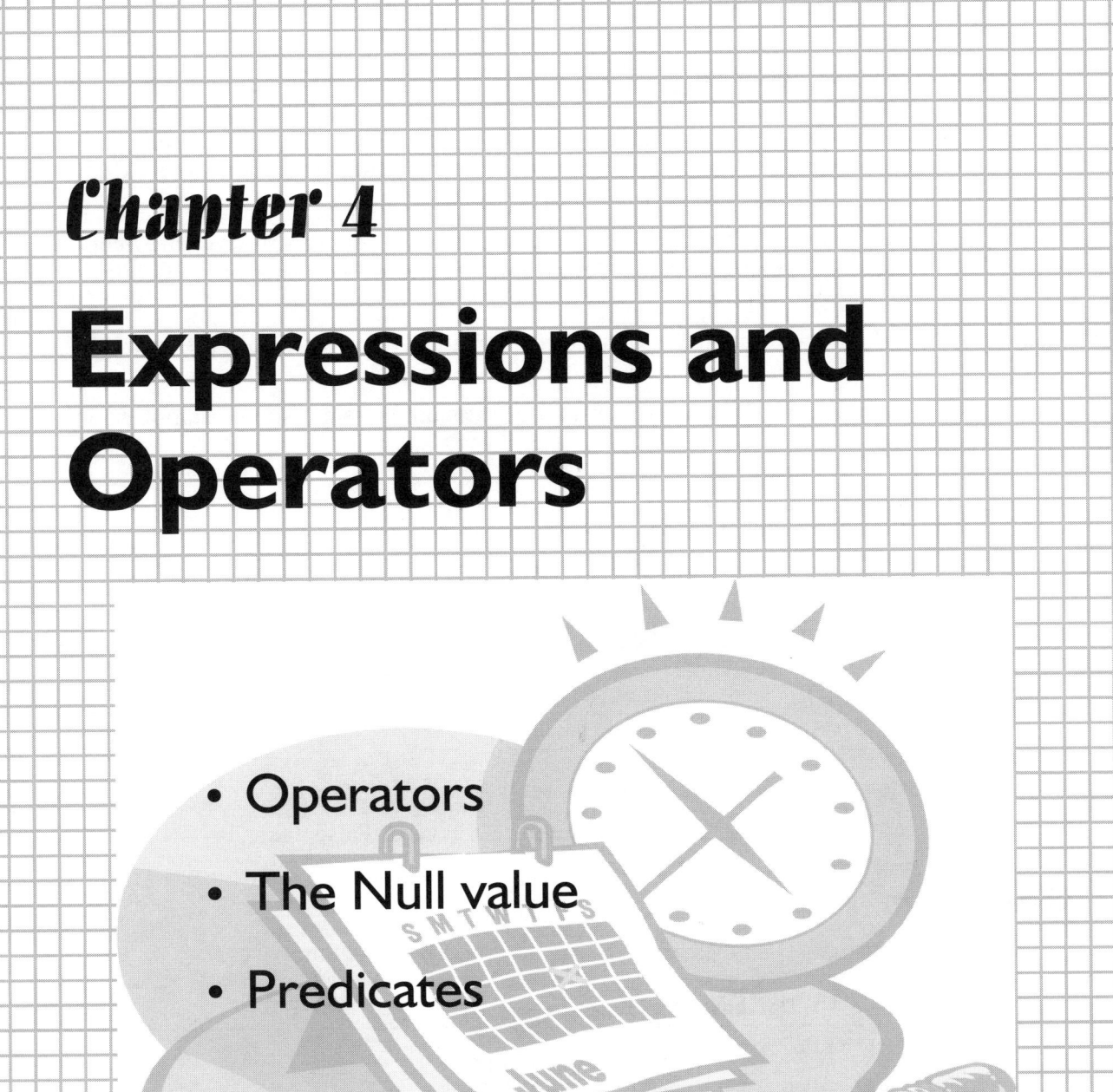

- Operators
- The Null value
- Predicates

To take advantage of a query created with the SELECT command you need to become familiar with expressions and operators. These are used to filter or perform operations on the data returned. Expressions are largely used in the SELECT command to compare the contents of fields.

Generally we can say that an *expression* is an item that generates a unique value or a combination of items and operators that returns a value. *Item* means the column name, a constant, a variable, the result of a function, or another expression.

When one of the items of a function contains the value Null, the expression will evaluate to null.

Operands and operators form an expression. Here are some examples:

State='TX'

Compares and checks if the contents of state is 'TX'.

X<>(25+3/2)

Analyzes and checks if the value of x is different from the sum of 25 and 1.5.

State = 'TX' OR 'CA'

Compares and checks if the contents of state is TX or CA.

All of these expressions will generate a True or False value.

Operators

These are the types of operators accepted by most databases:

Table 4-1. Database Operators

Arithmetic	
Multiplication	*
Division	/
Subtraction	–
Addition	+
Modulus	%

Table 4-1. Database Operators (continued)

Character	
Concatenation	||
Comparison	
Equal to	=
Not equal to	<>
Greater than	>
Less than	<
Greater than or equal to	>=
Less than or equal to	<=
Not less than	!<
Not greater than	!>
Not equal to	!=
Logical	
NOT	Inverts the Boolean value
AND	True when both expressions are true
OR	True when one expression is true
BETWEEN	True when the operand is within the range
LIKE	True when the operand finds a default
IN	True when some item is true
SOME	True when some item is true
ANY	True when any item is true
ALL	True when all the set is true
Bitwise	Perform bit manipulation operations between two integer expressions
&	Bitwise AND
|	Bitwise OR
^	Bitwise Exclusive OR
Unary	
+ (Positive)	The numeric value is positive
– (Negative)	The numeric value is negative
~ (Bitwise NOT)	Returns the complement of the number

Precedence of Operators

There are several types of operators. When more than one type of operator is present in an expression, they are evaluated according to a specific order, as described below:

1. + (Positive), − (Negative), ~ (Bitwise NOT)
2. * (Multiplication), / (Division), % (Modulus)
3. + (Addition), || (Concatenation), − (Subtraction)
4. =, >, <, >=, <=, , !=, !>, !< (Comparison)
5. ^ (Bitwise Exclusive OR), & (Bitwise AND), | (Bitwise OR)
6. NOT
7. AND
8. ALL, ANY, BETWEEN, IN, LIKE, OR, SOME
9. = (assignment)

Operators at the same level are evaluated from left to right. Using parentheses changes the precedence order, giving the expression within a higher priority.

The Null Value

A null value is not less than, nor equal to, nor greater than the value specified in the search condition. The null value is unknown (false). In these situations you must use the NULL predicate, which is discussed later in this section. Be careful when using a search condition that may have a null value in one of its rows, as it may return odd results.

```
SELECT * FROM table_name WHERE table_name IS NULL
```

Predicates

A predicate in a HAVING or WHERE clause is a search condition that may be true, false, or unknown. A predicate uses operators, expressions, and constants to specify the search condition. The main predicates are:

- Relational
- BETWEEN
- NULL
- EXISTS
- LIKE
- IN

Relational Predicates

There are two types of relational predicates: comparison and quantification predicates.

The comparison predicates compare one value to another, based on the relational operators. The simplest form of this predicate is represented by two expressions connected by one operator.

```
SELECT * FROM authors WHERE state= 'CA';
```

```
SELECT * FROM emp WHERE hiredate <= '1-Jan-1999';
```

```
SELECT * FROM emp WHERE salary >2500
```

The BETWEEN Predicate

This predicate compares the value inside a range of specified values.

```
SELECT * FROM emp WHERE salary BETWEEN 30000 AND 60000;
```

The figure below is an example in which the BETWEEN predicate filters records in the Sales table.

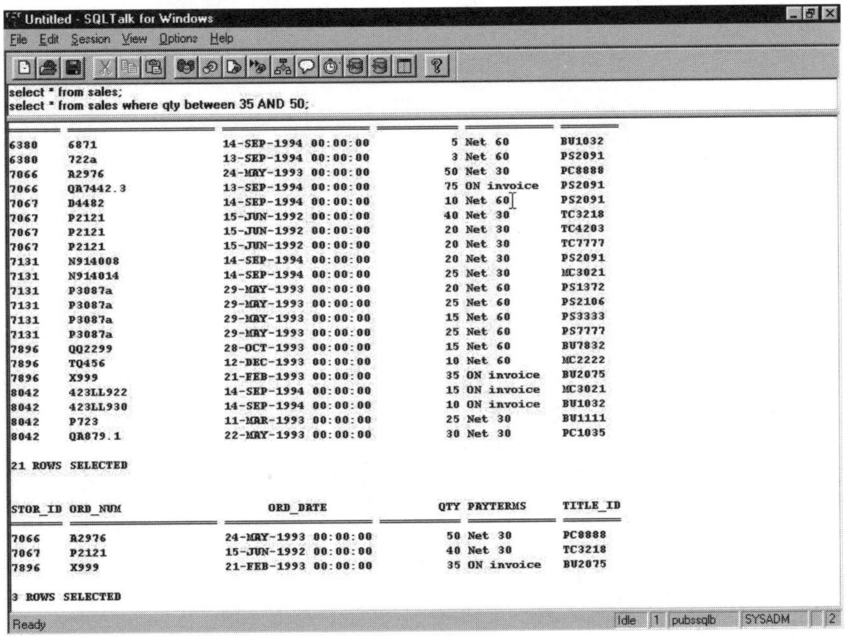

The NULL Predicate

The NULL predicate tests the existence of Null values.

SELECT * FROM emp WHERE deptno IS NULL;

As an example we will insert two more records in the Demo2 table created in the previous chapter. Then we will try to find the records with the Null values.

Input:

```
SELECT * FROM demo2;
INSERT INTO demo2 values(6,'sixth record', null);
INSERT INTO demo2 values(6,'seventh record', null);
SELECT * FROM demo2;
SELECT * FROM demo2 WHERE state IS NULL;
SELECT * FROM demo2 WHERE state='';
```

Result:

```
CODE    NAME            STATE
====    =============   =====
2       second record   WA
4       fourth record   CA
5       fifth record    LA

CODE    NAME            STATE
====    =============   =====
6       sixth record
2       second record   WA
4       fourth record   CA
5       fifth record    LA
6       seventh record

CODE    NAME            STATE
====    =============   =====
6       sixth record
6       seventh record

CODE    NAME            STATE
====    =============   =====

0 ROWS SELECTED
```

The EXISTS Predicate

This predicate tests the existence of certain rows inside the table. We will discuss this predicate in more detail later in Chapter 10. In the following example, we have selected the names of the publishers that have books listed in the Titles table. Although there are at least eight publishers, only three of them have books listed in this table.

This query reads the first record of the Publishers table, which is the code 0736 (see below). Then it checks the Titles table to see if it contains the same code in the pub_id field. If it exists, it returns the name and code fields from the Publishers table. Then it reads the second row of the Publishers table and repeats the search.

```
PUB_ID   PUB_NAME                CITY           STATE    COUNTRY
======   ====================    ==========     =====    =======
0736     New Moon Books          Boston         MA       USA
0877     Binnet & Hardley        Washington     DC       USA
1389     Algodata Infosystems    Berkeley       CA       USA
1622     Five Lakes Publishing   Chicago        IL       USA
1756     Ramona Publishers       Dallas         TX       USA
9901     GGG&G                   Munchen                 Germany
9952     Scootney Books          New York       NY       USA
9999     Lucerne Publishing      Paris                   France
```

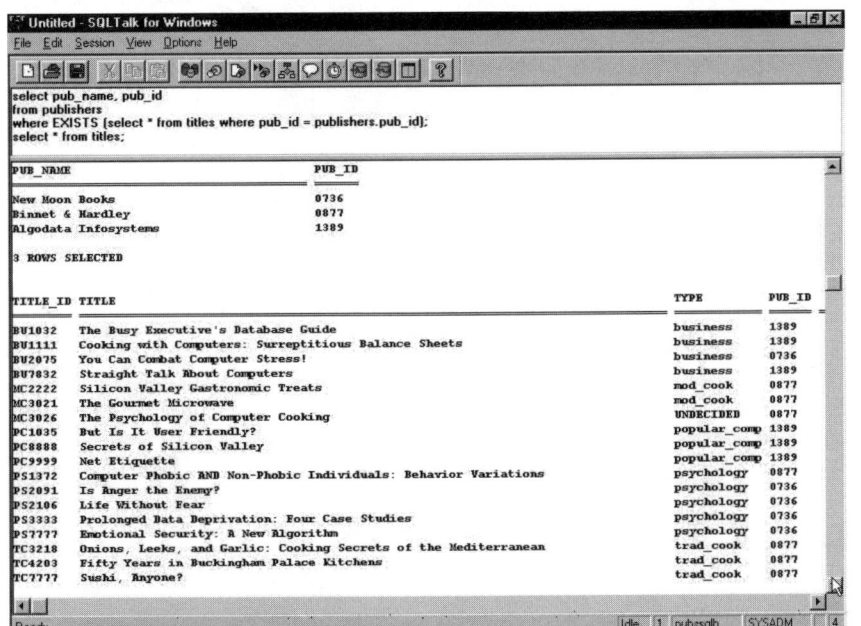

The LIKE Predicate

This predicate searches for strings of text that belong to the specified default. It can only be used in char or varchar type fields.

Its syntax is:

```
SEARCH expression [NOT] LIKE search_default
```

In the search default, the following characters can be used:

_ Underscore   Replaces the letter in its position
% Percentage   Replaces all the characters from that position on
\ Backslash   Represents the % sign

In the example on the next page we first searched for all the authors with first names beginning with C. Then we searched for all the authors who live in states that begin with the letter M. Finally, we searched for all the authors who live in states that begin with letters other than C.

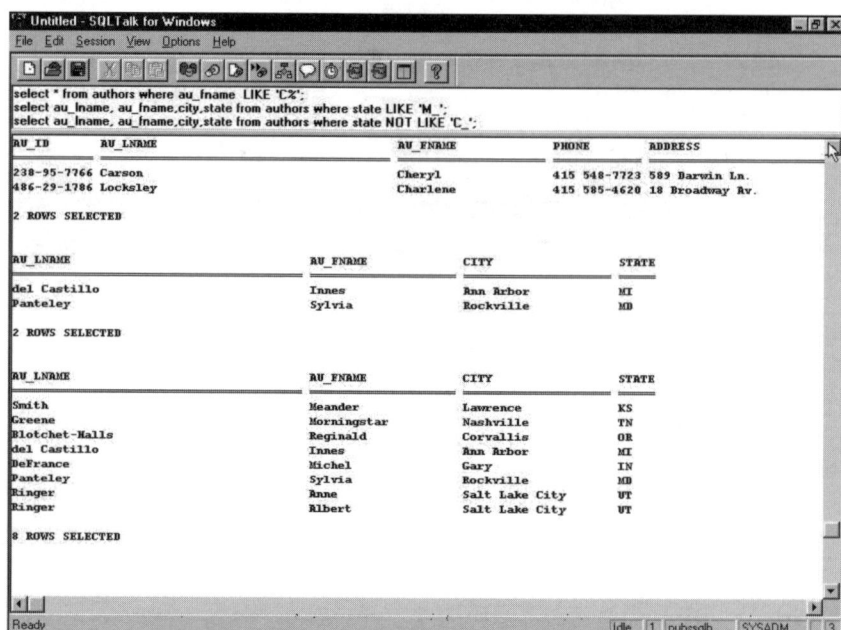

The IN Predicate

This predicate compares a value against a collection or list of values. Its syntax is:

```
test_expression IN (value1, value2, valueN, ...)
```

When there is just one element you do not need the parentheses.

The next example searches for authors who live in four states. The search found three authors who live in two of the states on the list.

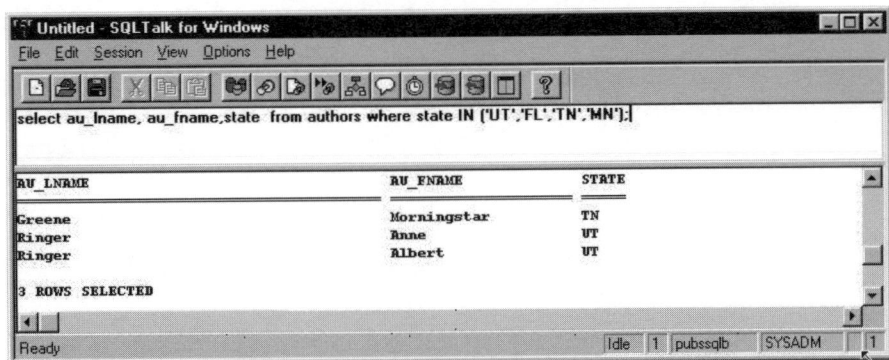

This predicate replaces the use of the logical operator OR when there are several conditions. Here is the same example using OR:

```
SELECT au_lname, au_fname, state FROM authors WHERE state='UT' OR
state='FL' OR state='TN' OR state='MN';
```

Summary

In this chapter you learned about expressions and predicates, which are fundamental for the construction of complex queries. In the next chapter we will see how to use expressions in columns and multiple tables.

Review Questions

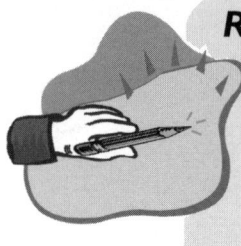

1. What is an expression?
2. What are the components of an expression?
3. What are the six types of operators?
4. What is a predicate?
5. What is the purpose of the NULL predicate?
6. What is the purpose of the EXISTS predicate?
7. What is the purpose of the IN predicate?
8. What is the purpose of the LIKE predicate?

Chapter 5
Expressions, Columns, and Multiple Tables

- The AS clause
- Calculated columns
- Creating aliases

48 ■ Chapter 5

The previous chapter gave an overview of expressions and operators. This chapter will show some practical uses of these elements in SELECT commands, which use the expressions together or in the place of column names, and in searches of tables.

Showing Alternate Column Names

When you run a SELECT command specifying some columns, the result is shown with the name of the field that is being used as the column name. Sometimes these names are of little help to the user because they may be named in a way that does not reflect their contents clearly. It is best to use a logical name so that others are able to read the query without trying to figure out what data the column contains.

Here is a simple example:

Input:

```
SELECT pub_id, pub_name FROM publishers WHERE country<>'USA';
```

Result:

```
PUB_ID   PUB_NAME
======   ==================
9901     GGG&G
9999     Lucerne Publishing
```

By using the AS clause after the column name, we can create an alias that will be used in the column's header. The next example replaces pub_id with Code and pub_name with Name.

Input:

```
SELECT pub_id AS Code, pub_name AS Name FROM publishers WHERE country<>'USA'
```

Result:

```
Code   Name
====   ==================
9901   GGG&G
9999   Lucerne Publishing
```

Joining Character Fields

A common practice is to show the contents of two columns as if they were only one item. The Authors table has the author's name divided into two columns: au_lname for the last name and au_fname for the first name. Using the string concatenation operator formed by two vertical bars (||), we can join those two columns. The next example uses this operator, which inserts a blank space between the two fields. The example also creates an alias for the column. Without this alias the column would have the expression "au_fname|| ' ' || au_lname" as its header.

Input:

```
SELECT au_fname|| ' ' || au_lname AS name FROM authors;
```

Result:

```
NAME
================
Johnson White
Marjorie Green
Cheryl Carson
Michael O'Leary
Dean Straight
Meander Smith
Abraham Bennet
Ann Dull
```

Showing Strings of Text Together with the Result

In addition to the contents of a column, the list of results can show strings of characters or calculated fields based on other columns. In the next example we create a phrase for each row in the table. The phrase is "The author X lives in city," where in the place of "X" we put the name from the au_lname column and in the place of "city" we use the contents of the City column.

Input:

```
SELECT 'The author', au_lname , 'lives in', city FROM authors;
```

Result:

```
'THE AUTHOR'     AU_LNAME      'LIVES IN'    CITY
============     ========      ==========    ==========
The author       White         lives in      Menlo Park
The author       Green         lives in      Oakland
The author       Carson        lives in      Berkeley
The author       O'Leary       lives in      San Jose
The author       Straight      lives in      Oakland
The author       Smith         lives in      Lawrence
The author       Bennet        lives in      Berkeley
```

Note that in this case the text is separated from the name of the column by a comma; this makes the program treat each element as if it were one distinct column.

Showing Calculated Columns

The SQL language allows the creation of calculated columns generated by an expression involving the contents of other columns. For example, let's say you want to know the current sales of computer books. First, we will see what the available books are:

Input:

```
SELECT title_id, price, ytd_sales, type FROM titles WHERE
type='popular_comp';
```

Result:

```
TITLE_ID   PRICE   YTD_SALES    TYPE
========   =====   =========    ============
PC1035     22.95   8780         popular_comp
PC8888     20      4095         popular_comp
PC9999                          popular_comp

3 ROWS SELECTED
```

Now we will add a calculated column that will show the total revenue generated by the sales of each book. To do that, we will create a column that multiplies the price of the book by the total sales of the book up to the present date (ytd_sales).

Input:

```
SELECT title_id, price, ytd_sales, price*ytd_sales, type FROM titles
WHERE type='popular_comp';
```

Result:

```
TITLE_ID  PRICE   YTD_SALES    PRICE*YTD_SALES   TYPE
========  =====   =========    ===============   ============
PC1035    22.95   8780         201501            popular_comp
PC8888    20      4095         81900             popular_comp
PC9999                                           popular_comp

3 ROWS SELECTED
```

In the next example we will create a query to show the prices of books if the price were to increase 10%.

Input:

```
SELECT title_id, price AS Actual, price*1.10 AS New, type FROM titles
WHERE type='popular_comp';
```

Result:

```
TITLE_ID  Actual  New     TYPE
========  ======  ======  ============
PC1035    22.95   25.245  popular_comp
PC8888    20      22      popular_comp
PC9999                    popular_comp
```

Creating Aliases for Table Names

When you create a query that shows the columns of more than one table, you must identify to which table each column belongs. This is done by specifying the table name, followed by a period and the name of the column. For example:

Titles.price
Authors.au_lname
Titles.pub_id
Publishers.pub_id

Different tables often have the same column name. Chapter 9 will cover in detail how to work with several tables, but for now, the following example shows all the codes of the books in the Titles table, and the publisher's name found in the Publishers table. Here, the Publishers table is searched for each row of the Titles table that shows the publisher code (pub_id) that is unique to the publisher code (pub_id) contained in the row of the Titles table.

Input:

```
SELECT titles.title_id, publishers.pub_name FROM titles, publishers
WHERE titles.pub_id = publishers.pub_id;
```

Result:

```
TITLES.TITLE_ID     PUBLISHERS.PUB_NAME
===============     ===================
BU2075              New Moon Books
PS2091              New Moon Books
PS2106              New Moon Books
PS3333              New Moon Books
PS7777              New Moon Books
MC2222              Binnet & Hardley
MC3021              Binnet & Hardley
MC3026              Binnet & Hardley
PS1372              Binnet & Hardley
TC3218              Binnet & Hardley
TC4203              Binnet & Hardley
TC7777              Binnet & Hardley
BU1032              Algodata Infosystems
BU1111              Algodata Infosystems
BU7832              Algodata Infosystems
PC1035              Algodata Infosystems
PC8888              Algodata Infosystems
PC9999              Algodata Infosystems
```

The more fields and tables used in a query, the more extensive the declaration. To save typing, you can create aliases for the tables used in the query, putting a name or alias immediately after the table name in the FROM clause. This alias can be used before the name of the column, instead of the complete name of the table.

The next example produces the same results as the above example. Here, we create the alias "p" for the Publishers table and "t" for the Titles table.

Input:

```
SELECT t.title_id, p.pub_name FROM titles t, publishers p WHERE
t.pub_id = p.pub_id;
```

Summary

In this chapter you created more useful queries by using alternate column headers, creating calculated fields, and concatenating the columns using aliases. The next chapter shows how to work with functions and aggregate functions.

Review Questions

1. Create a SELECT command which shows the titles Name for a column called emp_name and Code for a column called emp_code from a table named Emp.
2. What operator is used to concatenate two text strings?
3. Create a SELECT command which shows the text "*CITY* is the hometown of *AUTHOR*," where *CITY* is the city column and *AUTHOR* the au_fname column of the Author table.
4. Create a SELECT command which shows a calculated field using the Title table. Show the title, code, price, ytd_sales, and the royalties (10% of the total sales).
5. What is the advantage of using a table alias in a SELECT command?

Day 2

Chapter

6—Functions

7—Ordering Results

8—Grouping Data

9—Joining Tables

10—Subqueries

Chapter 6
Functions

- Types of functions
- The DISTINCT clause

A SQL function is a routine that performs a specific operation and returns a result. It is similar to a procedure, except that procedures do not return any value. A function can receive arguments that are used in processing.

The basic syntax of a function is:

Funcname(arg1,arg2,...argn)

Funcname is the name of the function, such as ABS or LOWER. Arg1 and arg2 are the optional parameters of the function.

Types of Functions

The SQL functions are categorized as single row, or scalar, functions and group, or aggregate, functions. A single row type function returns the result for each row in a table or view. A group type function returns only one result for a group of rows.

For example, the function LOWER( ) converts its argument to lowercase. The function UPPER( ) converts the argument to uppercase. These functions can be used in SELECT commands that have the WHERE clause, but they cannot be used with GROUP BY.

All database vendors have added their own functions to expand their product's capabilities. Many functions are common to most dialects. However, before using a function see Appendix A, which lists the functions and the dialects they work in. SQLBase requires the use of the @ sign before the name of a function. While SQL Server 7 and Oracle use UPPER for the function that converts a string to uppercase, SQLBase uses @UPPER, as shown in the following example. The example also shows the LEFT function, which displays the first *n* characters of a string. In this example, just the first eight positions from the left in the City field are displayed.

Input:

SELECT @upper(au_lname), @left(city, 8) FROM authors WHERE state<>'CA';

Result:

```
@UPPER(AU_LNAME)    @LEFT(CITY,8)
================    =============
SMITH               Lawrence
GREENE              Nashvill
BLOTCHET-HALLS      Corvalli
DEL CASTILLO        Ann Arbo
```

```
DEFRANCE        Gary
PANTELEY        Rockvill
RINGER          Salt Lak
RINGER          Salt Lak
```

This chapter will focus on the standard aggregate functions. The specific functions of each dialect are listed in the appendixes.

Aggregate Functions

The group, or aggregate, functions process a group of rows in the table and return the result. Most of these functions act on all the rows as the default; however, they can be applied to a group of rows. Generally, they compute a summary value based on the contents of the group of rows.

The types of data that can be processed by these functions are numeric, character, or date.

They accept the following parameters:

DISTINCT   Makes the function act only on the rows that have different values.

ALL   Makes the function consider all the values (rows), including the duplicates. This is the default.

With the exception of the COUNT function, the others ignore null values.

The aggregate functions are AVG, COUNT, MAX, MIN, and SUM. On the following page is an explanation of what each function does.

AVG

Returns the arithmetic average for *n*.

`AVG([DISTINCT|ALL] n)`

COUNT

Returns the number of rows of the query. *Expr* represents the non-null field or expression.

`COUNT({* | [DISTINCT|ALL] expr})`

MAX

Returns the maximum value for *expr*.

`MAX([DISTINCT|ALL] expr)`

MIN

Returns the minimum value for *expr*.

MIN([DISTINCT|ALL] expr)

SUM

Returns the sum of values in the expression.

SUM([DISTINCT|ALL] expr)

Following are several examples of these functions. The first example displays four columns corresponding to the average, maximum value, minimum value, and sum of the ytd_sales field (the number of books sold in the year) of the Titles table in the Pubssqlb database. First we will list all of the table's rows to check the result of the aggregate functions:

Input:

SELECT title_id, ytd_sales FROM titles;

Result:

```
TITLE_ID  YTD_SALES
========  =========
BU1032    4095
BU1111    3876
BU2075    18722
BU7832    4095
MC2222    2032
MC3021    22246
MC3026
PC1035    8780
PC8888    4095
PC9999
PS1372    375
PS2091    2045
PS2106    111
PS3333    4072
PS7777    3336
TC3218    375
TC4203    15096
TC7777    4095
18 ROWS SELECTED
```

Now we will use some aggregate functions. They process, individually, the ytd_sale field of all the rows and show the final result. When you specify an aggregate function, you cannot use other fields in the list of fields; otherwise an error will occur.

Input:

```
SELECT AVG(ytd_sales), MAX(ytd_sales), MIN(ytd_sales), SUM(ytd_sales)
FROM titles;
```

Result:

AVG(YTD_SALES)	MAX(YTD_SALES)	MIN(YTD_SALES)	SUM(YTD_SALES)
6090.375	22246	111	97446

1 ROW SELECTED

The COUNT function can be used as an argument with the name of a column or with an asterisk to process all rows of the table. This function acts differently when it finds rows with a null value. This example shows the total number of records in the Titles table:

Input:

```
SELECT COUNT(*) FROM titles;
```

Result:

```
COUNT(*)
========
18
```

The next example returns just those rows with a value other than null for the Advance field. If you check the table in Appendix F you will see that two rows have no value in this field.

Input:

```
SELECT COUNT(advance) FROM titles;
```

Result:

```
COUNT(ADVANCE)
==============
16
```

The next example tells how many books will have a royalty payment, i.e., how many rows have a value different from null for this column:

Input:

```
SELECT COUNT(royalty) FROM titles;
```

Result:

```
COUNT(ROYALTY)
==============
16
```

1 ROW SELECTED

Using the DISTINCT Clause

Using the DISTINCT clause as an aggregate function eliminates the rows with identical values before performing the function.

The next example gives the number of types of royalties, showing the number of distinct values inside the Royalty column.

Input:

```
SELECT COUNT(distinct royalty)
FROM titles;
```

Result:

```
COUNT(DISTINCT ROYALTY)
=======================
5
```

1 ROW SELECTED

The use of DISTINCT requires careful planning, as the results may be incorrect since the aggregate functions do not consider rows with null values. The next example shows the total, average, and sum of the Price column. Since two rows have a null value, only 16 rows are considered.

Input:

```
SELECT COUNT(price), AVG(price), SUM(price) FROM titles;
```

Result:

```
COUNT(PRICE)    AVG(PRICE)    SUM(PRICE)
============    ==========    ==========
16              14.76625      236.26
```

1 ROW SELECTED

If you want to find out the number of different prices, the average of these different prices, and their sum, you must use the DISTINCT option in every function.

Input:

```
SELECT COUNT(DISTINCT price), AVG(DISTINCT price), SUM(DISTINCT price)
FROM titles;
```

Result:

```
COUNT(DISTINCT PRICE)    AVG(DISTINCT PRICE)    SUM(DISTINCT PRICE)
=====================    ===================    ===================
11                       14.66818182            161.35
```

Use Restrictions

You cannot use an aggregate function in a WHERE clause. However, you can use the WHERE clause to restrict the number of rows that will be considered by the aggregate functions. The next example first shows the average value of the books. Then it displays the average value of business books and computer books.

Input:

```
SELECT AVG(price) FROM titles;
SELECT AVG(price) FROM titles WHERE type='business';
SELECT AVG(price) FROM titles WHERE type='popular_comp';
```

Result:

```
AVG(PRICE)
==========
14.76625
```

1 ROW SELECTED

```
AVG(PRICE)
==========
13.73

1 ROW SELECTED

AVG(PRICE)
==========
21.475

1 ROW SELECTED
```

Summary

The aggregate functions are crucial for creating queries that require the summarization of rows and data groups in a table. The specialized functions and characteristics of each database extend the functionality of the language, but also contribute to the incompatibility between the many databases available in the market. If you plan to create multi-platform applications, check first for the compatibility or correlation of the functions among the dialects used. In the next chapter we will discuss how to order the results of a table.

Review Questions

1. What is a function?
2. What are the types of functions?
3. What is the purpose of the aggregate functions?
4. What is the purpose of the DISTINCT clause?
5. Create a SELECT command to show the number of job titles.
6. Create a SELECT command to show the average salary for particular job titles.

Chapter 7
Ordering Results

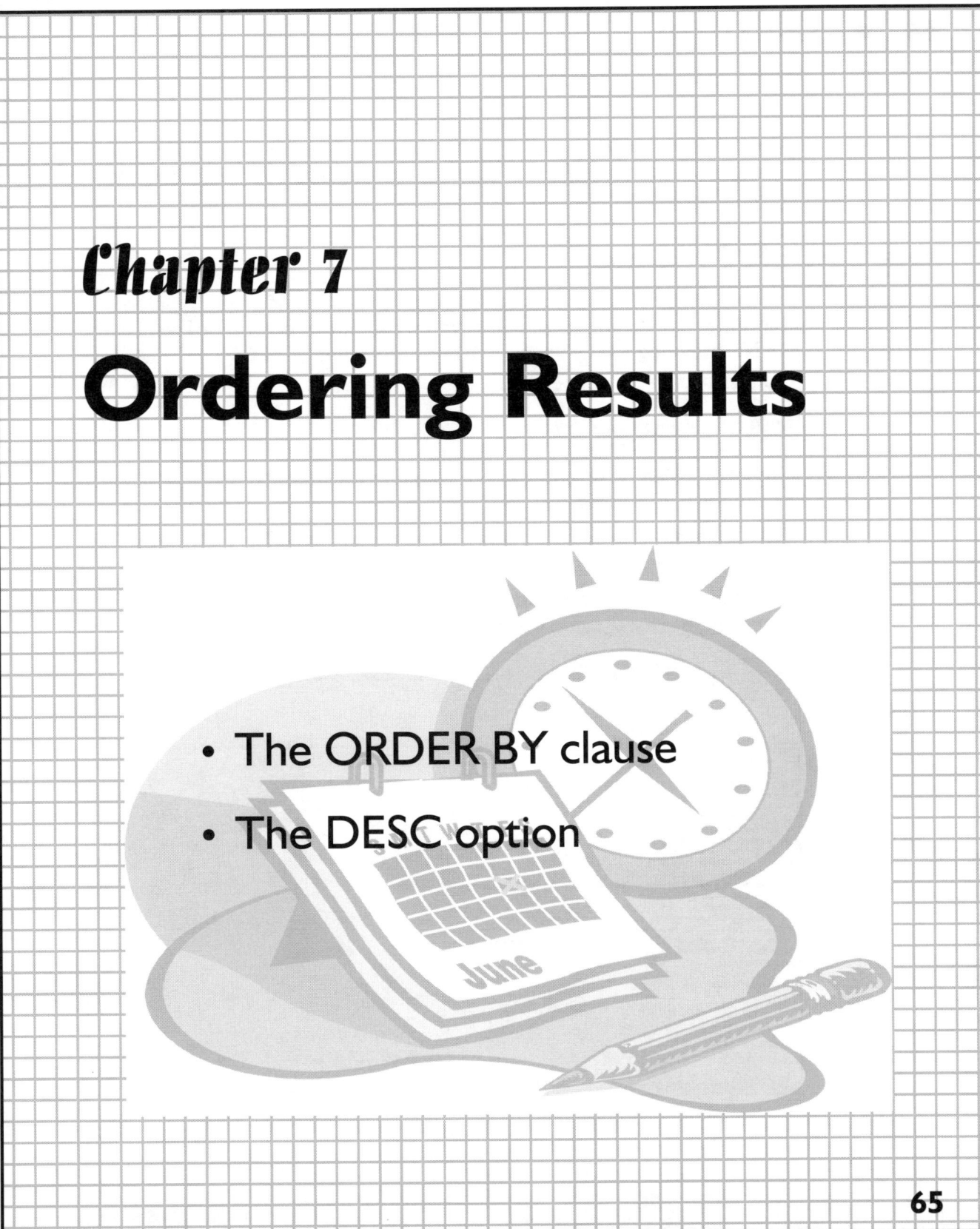

- The ORDER BY clause
- The DESC option

The results returned by a query are based on the physical order of the tables or on the indexes that are active during the execution of the query. However, you can specify how the rows are displayed by using the ORDER BY clause.

The ORDER BY Clause

The ORDER BY clause forces the database to return the rows organized according to the contents of one or more columns. The order of display can be ascending (ASC, the default) or descending (DESC).

The syntax is:

```
ORDER BY <expression> [<ASC>| <DESC> position]
```

where *expression* is the name of the column or an expression used to create the calculated column.

Most database systems require that the expression used in ORDER BY appear in the list of columns of the SELECT command.

The following figure shows the natural order of the query results:

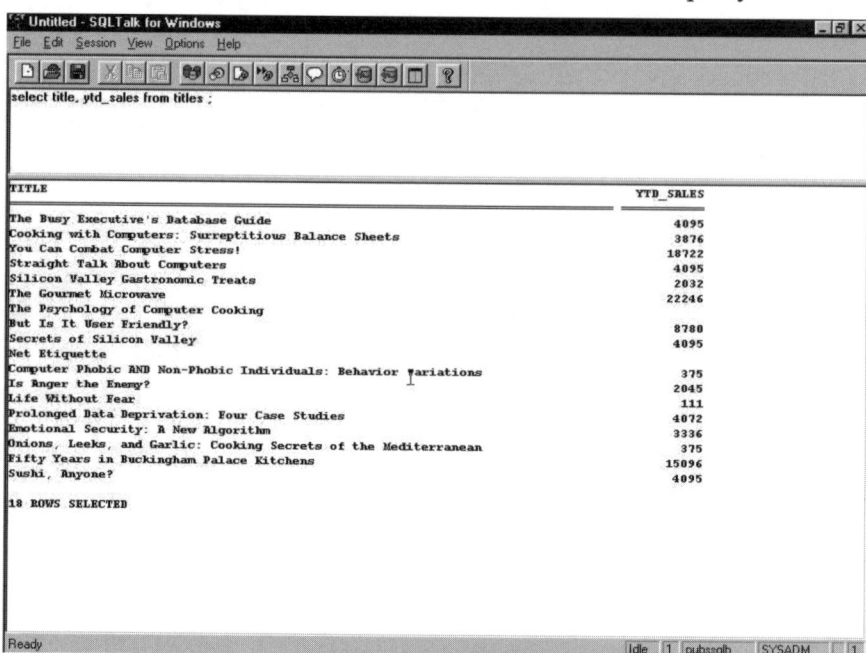

Using the ORDER BY clause we can quickly alphabetize the titles as shown below.

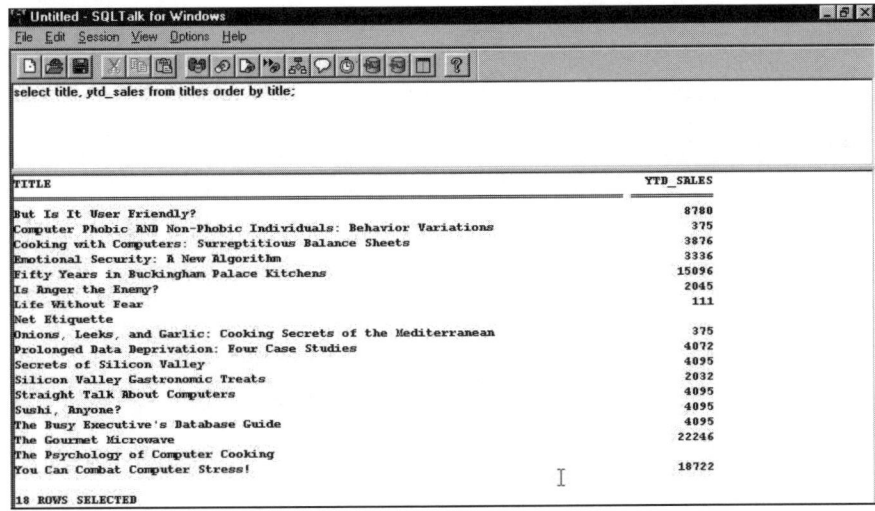

Descending Order

As mentioned previously, by default the results are displayed in ascending order. To list the rows in reverse order you must add the DESC option to the ORDER BY clause. In the example below, the books are listed in descending order of sales:

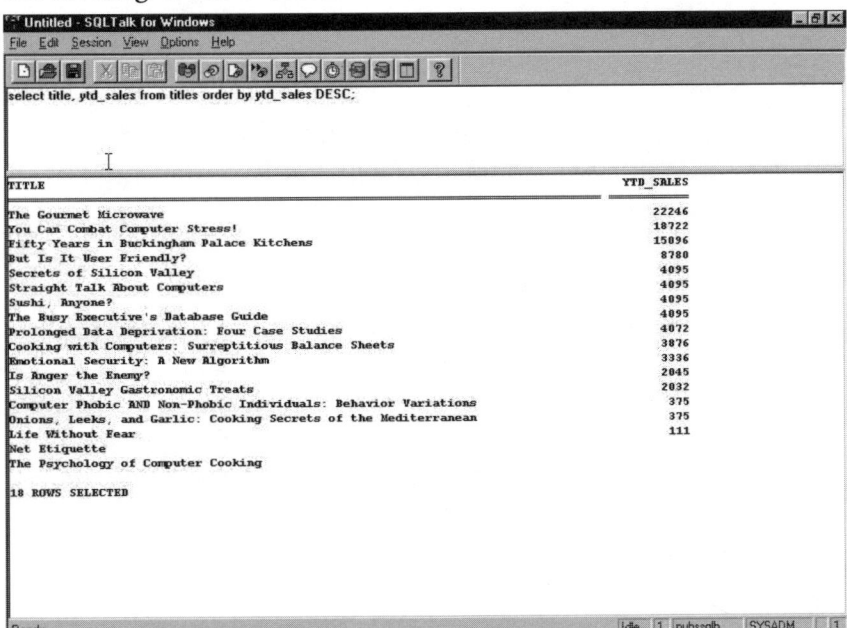

The sort order is determined by the set of characters installed and by the default sort order adopted by the database. What happens when there are two names such as Antonio and antonio? Which one will appear first? Here we have some examples that can be configured depending on the language and the database used:

Dictionary order, case insensitive	A = a, Ä = ä, Å = å, a ≠ à ≠ á ≠ â ≠ ä ≠ å, A ≠ Ä ≠ Å	a, A, à, á, â, ä, Ä, Å, å
Dictionary order, case sensitive	A ≠ a, Ä ≠ ä, Å ≠ å, a ≠ à ≠ á ≠ â ≠ ä ≠ å, A ≠ Ä ≠ Å	A, a, à, á, â, Ä, ä, Å, å
Dictionary order, case insensitive, uppercase preference	A = a, Ä = ä, Å = å, a ≠ à ≠ á ≠ â ≠ ä ≠ å, A ≠ Ä ≠ Å	A, a, à, á, â, Ä, ä, Å, å
Dictionary order, case insensitive, accent insensitive	A = a = à = á = â = Ä = ä = Å = å	a, A, à, â, á, Ä, ä, Å, å

Check your database/operating system manual to determine the sort order used.

Restrictions

You cannot use ORDER BY with a SELECT command that is part of a UNION of SELECT commands. ORDER BY also cannot be used in the definition of a view or in a subquery.

Ordering By More Than One Column

The ORDER BY clause allows you to order by more than one column or expression. In this case you just specify the columns or expressions separated by commas. The order of the columns in the ORDER BY clause indicates the order of organization. The data is ordered by the first column specified, then by the second column specified, and so on. In the following example are three columns from the Titles table listed in their natural order.

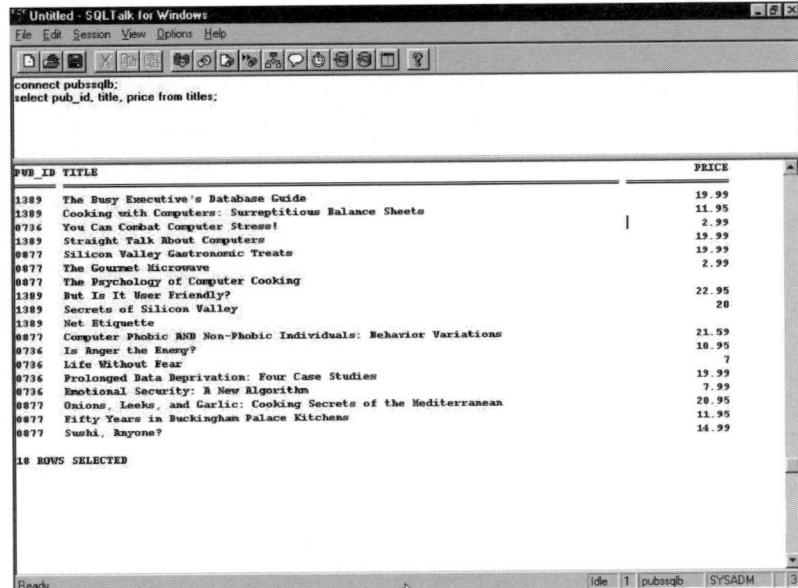

In the next example we use ORDER BY with pub_id and Title to organize the results. The rows are first organized by publisher (pub_id) and then by title (Title). That is, the publishers are listed by number in ascending order, and within each group the titles are listed in alphabetical order.

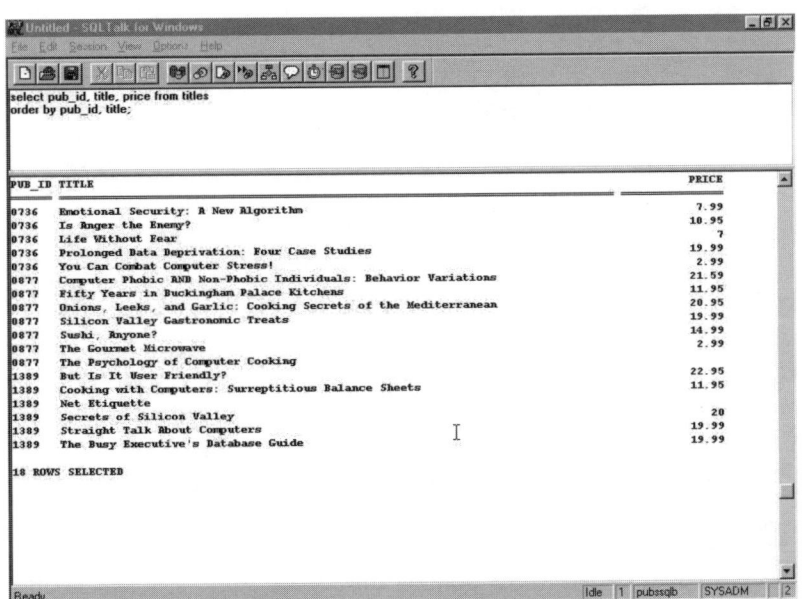

Ordering Using Expressions

The ORDER BY clause allows you to organize a list of results through calculated columns by using expressions. In this case, you can reference the calculated column in two ways: by specifying its position number inside the list of columns and through the creation and use of an alias for the column.

In this example, the third column is an expression that returns the total sales of the book.

Input:

```
SELECT pub_id, title_id, price*ytd_sales FROM titles
ORDER BY 3;
```

Here is the result:

```
PUB_ID   TITLE_ID  PRICE*YTD_SALES
======   ========  ===============
0877     MC3026
1389     PC9999
0736     PS2106    777
0877     TC3218    7856.25
0877     PS1372    8096.25
0736     PS2091    22392.75
0736     PS7777    26654.64
0877     MC2222    40619.68
1389     BU1111    46318.2
0736     BU2075    55978.78
0877     TC7777    61384.05
0877     MC3021    66515.54
0736     PS3333    81399.28
1389     BU1032    81859.05
1389     BU7832    81859.05
1389     PC8888    81900
0877     TC4203    180397.2
1389     PC1035    201501

18 ROWS SELECTED
```

Note that the fields with a null value appear first.

Note Not all database systems behave the same. Some systems group the nulls at the beginning of the list, regardless of the sort order.

Ordering Using the Column Header

Using the same example as above, we will create an alias for the calculated column and use this alias in ORDER BY.

Note: Not all database systems accept this option. This example is valid for SQL Server 7.

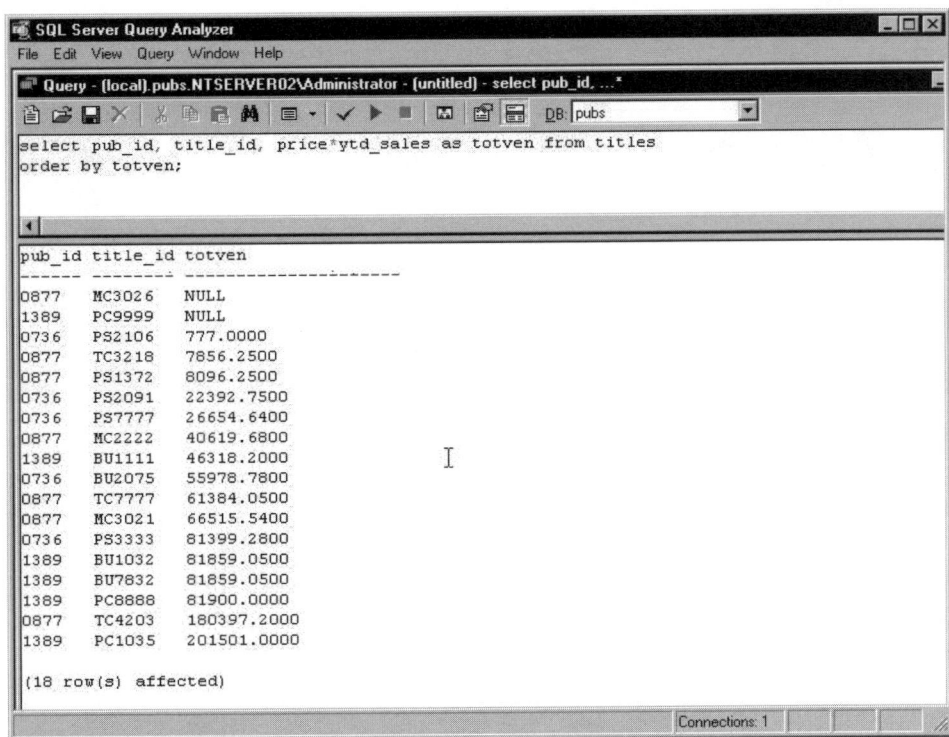

Summary

This chapter showed how to use the ORDER BY clause to organize query results, based on a column or expression. In the next chapter we will see how to group data using the GROUP BY clause.

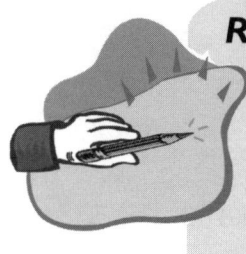

Review Questions

1. What is the purpose of the ORDER BY clause?
2. In what order are the results of the ORDER BY clause shown?
3. How do you show the results in descending order?
4. How do you order by two or more columns?
5. If you specify more than one column, what order of precedence is used?

Chapter 8
Grouping Data

- The GROUP BY clause
- The WHERE clause
- The HAVING clause

In the previous chapter we saw how to order the results of a SELECT command using ORDER BY. We have also seen how to obtain summary values of groups of rows using aggregate functions. The aggregate functions act either on the entire table or on part of the table by using the DISTINCT option. To expand the use of the aggregation you need to know how to group the rows of a table based on some criteria. This task is performed by the GROUP BY clause, which when combined with other clauses of the SELECT command allows the creation of powerful queries. With it you can answer questions such as "What categories of books are available and what is the total number of titles that each publisher has for this category of books?"

The GROUP BY Clause

You can list more than one column in GROUP BY, so as to nest groups of rows. You can also use the aggregate functions in GROUP BY. The basic syntax of this clause is:

```
GROUP BY column_list
```

Often, the effect obtained by GROUP BY can be obtained another way. The following two commands return the same result, i.e., a row for each publisher found in the Titles table.

Input:

```
SELECT DISTINCT pub_id FROM titles;

SELECT pub_id FROM titles
GROUP BY pub_id;
```

Result:

```
PUB_ID
======
0736
0877
1389

PUB_ID
======
0736
0877
1389
```

Now let's look at these two commands:

Input:

```
SELECT type, pub_id FROM titles ORDER BY type;

SELECT type, pub_id
FROM titles
GROUP BY type, pub_id;
```

Result:

```
TYPE            PUB_ID
=========       ======
UNDECIDED       0877
business        0736
business        1389
business        1389
business        1389
mod_cook        0877
mod_cook        0877
popular_comp    1389
popular_comp    1389
popular_comp    1389
psychology      0736
psychology      0736
psychology      0736
psychology      0736
psychology      0877
trad_cook       0877
trad_cook       0877
trad_cook       0877

18 ROWS SELECTED

TYPE            PUB_ID
=========       ======
UNKNOWN         0877
business        0736
business        1389
mod_cook        0877
popular_comp    1389
psychology      0736
psychology      0877
trad_cook       0877
```

The first command lists all the records in the table, ordering them by type. The second command uses GROUP BY to group the rows of each product type, as well as the publishers that have books in that category. Compare the two listings and note that the grouping is coherent. For example, only the publishers with the codes 0736 and 0877 have books about psychology. We can also see that publisher 0736 has one business title, while publisher 1389 has three.

The advantage of using GROUP BY is the ability to apply the aggregate functions to every group found, as shown below.

Input:

```
SELECT type, pub_id, COUNT(type), AVG(price), SUM(ytd_sales)
FROM titles
GROUP BY type, pub_id;
```

Result:

TYPE	PUB_ID	COUNT(TYPE)	AVG(PRICE)	SUM(YTD_SALES)
UNKNOWN	0877	1		
business	0736	1	2.99	18722
business	1389	3	17.31	12066
mod_cook	0877	2	11.49	24278
popular_comp	1389	3	21.475	12875
psychology	0736	4	11.4825	9564
psychology	0877	1	21.59	375
trad_cook	0877	3	15.9633333	19566

8 ROWS SELECTED

Note that we can summarize the data by type and publisher using the aggregate functions. Without GROUP BY you could only get this data by running individual queries.

Input:

```
SELECT COUNT(type), AVG(price), SUM(ytd_sales) FROM titles WHERE type='business' AND pub_id='1389';
```

Result:

COUNT(TYPE)	AVG(PRICE)	SUM(YTD_SALES)
3	17.31	12066

Using the WHERE Clause

You can use the combination of WHERE and GROUP BY in a SELECT command to filter the rows that will be grouped. The rows that do not satisfy the condition specified by WHERE are eliminated before the grouping is done.

Input:

```
SELECT type, AVG(price), AVG(advance)
FROM titles
WHERE advance > 7000
GROUP BY type;
```

Result:

```
TYPE            AVG(PRICE)   AVG(ADVANCE)
============    =========    ============
business        2.99         10125
mod_cook        2.99         15000
popular_comp    20           8000
trad_cook       14.99        8000

4 ROWS SELECTED
```

The Null Value

When a column used for grouping contains a null value, a group will be created for it in the result. In other words, all the rows containing null values are grouped. The display order of the group with null values depends on the particular database used.

In this example, the Royalty column in the Titles table contains some null values.

Input:

```
SELECT royalty, AVG(price)
FROM titles
GROUP BY royalty;
```

Result:

```
ROYALTY  AVG(PRICE)
=======  ==========
NULL     NULL
10       16.444
12       15.47
14       11.95
16       22.95
24       2.99
```

Some databases use the word NULL in the list of results. Others just leave it blank.

To eliminate groups based on null values you can use the WHERE clause, as in the next example:

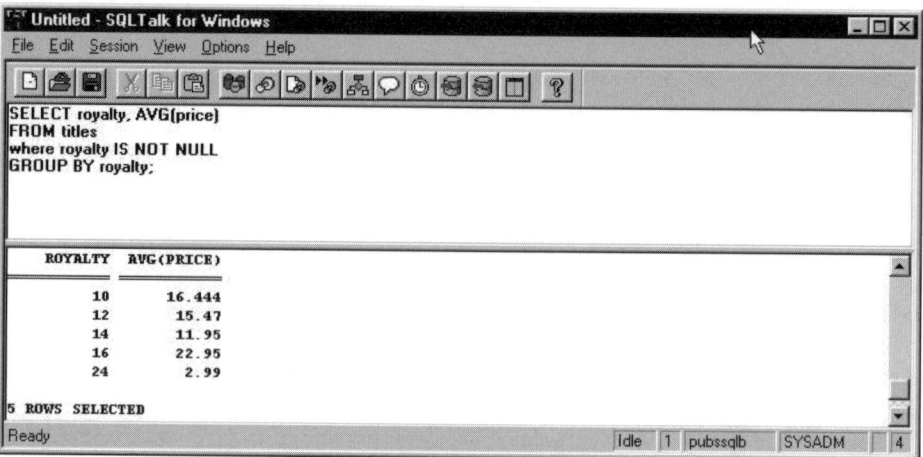

Using the HAVING Clause

While the WHERE clause filters records before grouping them, thus eliminating some records generated by GROUP BY, the HAVING clause filters the group of records already created. HAVING acts like WHERE, but it can have an aggregate function specified as a filter.

In the next example, HAVING is used to filter the result so only the publishers that have ytd_sales greater than 25,000 are displayed.

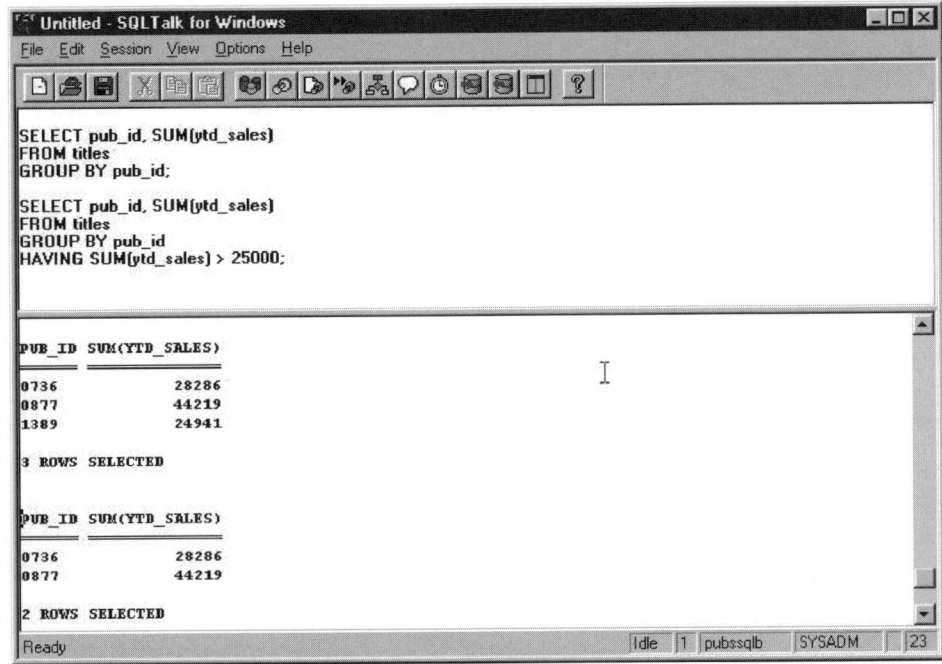

The WHERE clause is used to filter the rows that result from the query to the table specified by the FROM clause. The GROUP BY clause is used to group the rows filtered by WHERE. The HAVING clause is used to filter the rows of the group created by ORDER BY.

The next example shows the use of HAVING with an aggregate function. In this case, after computing all the groups, only those groups containing more than three books are displayed.

Input:

```
SELECT type
FROM titles
GROUP BY type
HAVING COUNT(*) > 3;
```

Result:

```
TYPE
============
business
psychology
```

You can obtain a similar filtering without the use of aggregate functions by using the LIKE predicate. As shown in the next example, only the types of books that start with the letter "p" are listed.

```
SELECT type
FROM titles
GROUP BY type
HAVING type LIKE 'p%';
```

Result:

```
TYPE
============
popular_comp
psychology

2 ROWS SELECTED
```

Using the ORDER BY Clause

The ORDER BY clause can be used to order the output of the results. Consider the next two groups of commands. The first uses ORDER BY and the second does not:

Input:

```
SELECT pub_id, SUM(advance) AS SUM, AVG(price)
FROM titles
GROUP BY pub_id
ORDER BY pub_id  DESC;

SELECT pub_id, SUM(advance) AS SUM, AVG(price)
FROM titles
GROUP BY pub_id;
```

Result:

PUB_ID	SUM	AVG(PRICE)
1389	30000	18.976
0877	41000	15.41
0736	24400	9.784

3 ROWS SELECTED

```
PUB_ID    SUM      AVG(PRICE)
======    =====    ==========
0736      24400    9.784
0877      41000    15.41
1389      30000    18.976
```

Following is an example that uses all the clauses we have seen so far. All the rows with a type beginning with the letter "p" and a price greater than $5 are selected. The rows are grouped by type and publisher (type and pub_id), where the sum of the advance is greater than $1,000, and the average price is greater than $12.

Input:

```
SELECT type, pub_id, SUM(advance), AVG(price)
FROM titles
WHERE type LIKE 'p%'
AND price >= 5
GROUP BY type, pub_id
HAVING SUM(advance) > 1000
AND AVG(price) >12
ORDER BY pub_id DESC;
```

Result:

```
TYPE            PUB_ID   SUM(ADVANCE)    AVG(PRICE)
============    ======   ============    ==========
popular_comp    1389     15000           21.475
psychology      0877     7000            21.59

2 ROWS SELECTED
```

Summary

A key element for mastering SQL is learning to use the clauses discussed in this chapter. They are responsible for creating sophisticated and complex queries. In the next chapter you will learn how to join tables so you can use data from more than one table.

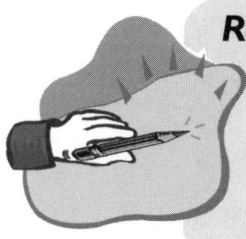

Review Questions

1. What is the purpose of the GROUP BY clause?
2. What happens if a column has null values?
3. What is the difference between the WHERE and HAVING clauses?
4. How do you order the result set?

Chapter 9
Joining Tables

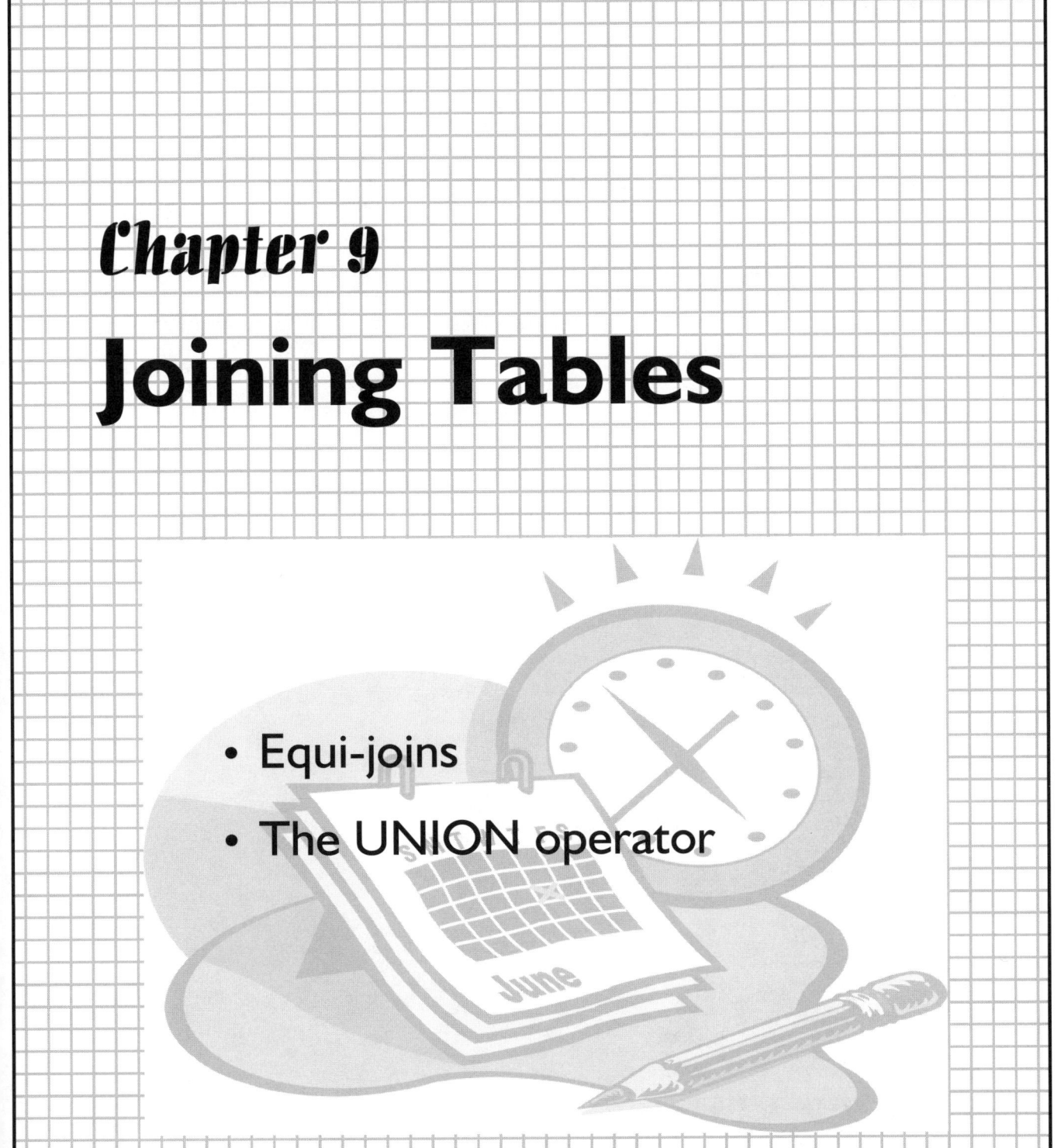

- Equi-joins
- The UNION operator

One of the most useful features of SQL is the ability to create relationships among tables in order to recover data from more than one with a single query. So far we have been working essentially with the recovery of data from one table. Through an operation called *joining* it is possible to see and manipulate data from more than one table using only one SELECT command.

Joining tables is a feature partially supported by SQL-92. However, many database vendors have implemented their own clauses. The most universal form of creating a join among tables uses the WHERE clause of the SELECT command.

How a Join Works

When planning to join two tables, you must consider how the joining works. When a SELECT command specifies fields in two tables without any restrictions or filters, the result will be a number of rows equivalent to the total rows of the first table multiplied by the total rows of the second table. This is because for each row of the first table all the rows of the second table are processed. Consider the contents of the Test5 and Test6 tables:

```
SELECT * FROM test5;
SELECT * FROM test6;

COL1TEST5        COL2TEST5
=========        =========
aaaa             1111
bbbb             2222
cccc             3333
dddd             4444

4 ROWS SELECTED

COL1TEST6        COL2TEST6
=========        =========
aaaa             1111
bbbb             2222
cccc             3333
dddd             4444

4 ROWS SELECTED
```

Input:

```
SELECT * FROM test5, test6;
```

Result:

COL1TEST5	COL2TEST5	COL1TEST6	COL2TEST6
=========	=========	=========	=========
aaaa	1111	aaaa	1111
bbbb	2222	aaaa	1111
cccc	3333	aaaa	1111
dddd	4444	aaaa	1111
aaaa	1111	bbbb	2222
bbbb	2222	bbbb	2222
cccc	3333	bbbb	2222
dddd	4444	bbbb	2222
aaaa	1111	cccc	3333
bbbb	2222	cccc	3333
cccc	3333	cccc	3333
dddd	4444	cccc	3333
aaaa	1111	dddd	4444
bbbb	2222	dddd	4444
cccc	3333	dddd	4444
dddd	4444	dddd	4444

16 ROWS SELECTED

The first row contains the first rows of each of the tables. The second row contains the second row of Test5 and the first row of Test6. The third row shows the third row of Test5 and the first row of Test6. All the rows of the first table are listed in association with the first row of the second table. Then, all the rows of the first table are listed in association with the second row of the second table, and so on. Thus, the result has 16 rows (4 rows of Test5 * 4 rows of Test6).

So when we use a simple command to list the title_id field from the Titles table and the pub_name field from the Publishers table we will have 144 rows (18 from Titles * 8 from Publishers).

Input:

```
SELECT title_id, pub_name FROM titles, publishers;
```

Result (partial):

```
TITLE_ID  PUB_NAME
========  ====================
BU1032    New Moon Books
BU1032    Binnet & Hardley
BU1032    Algodata Infosystems
BU1032    Five Lakes Publishing
BU1032    Ramona Publishers
BU1032    GGG&G
BU1032    Scootney Books
BU1032    Lucerne Publishing
BU1111    New Moon Books
BU1111    Binnet & Hardley
BU1111    Algodata Infosystems
BU1111    Five Lakes Publishing
BU1111    Ramona Publishers
BU1111    GGG&G
BU1111    Scootney Books
BU1111    Lucerne Publishing
BU2075    New Moon Books
BU2075    Binnet & Hardley
BU2075    Algodata Infosystems
...

144 ROWS SELECTED
```

This result is incorrect, since it shows that a book title seems to belong to each of the eight publishers.

A joining of tables only makes sense when you restrict the set of results with a WHERE clause, as in the example below.

Input:

```
SELECT title_id, pub_name FROM titles, publishers
WHERE titles.pub_id=publishers.pub_id;
```

Result:

```
TITLE_ID  PUB_NAME
========  ====================
BU2075    New Moon Books
PS2091    New Moon Books
PS2106    New Moon Books
PS3333    New Moon Books
PS7777    New Moon Books
```

```
MC2222      Binnet & Hardley
MC3021      Binnet & Hardley
MC3026      Binnet & Hardley
PS1372      Binnet & Hardley
TC3218      Binnet & Hardley
TC4203      Binnet & Hardley
TC7777      Binnet & Hardley
BU1032      Algodata Infosystems
BU1111      Algodata Infosystems
BU7832      Algodata Infosystems
PC1035      Algodata Infosystems
PC8888      Algodata Infosystems
PC9999      Algodata Infosystems

18 ROWS SELECTED
```

Creating an Equi-join

In previous chapters you have seen that it is possible to return data from more than one table using the SELECT command. In this case, each column must be preceded by the name of the table. In the FROM clause you must specify the tables separated by commas. You can create a join based on an equality, in which the fields of two tables have the same contents. This type of join is also called an *equi-join*.

Here is an example of an equi-join.

```
SELECT titles.title, publishers.pub_name
FROM titles, publishers
WHERE titles.pub_id=publishers.pub_id;
```

This SELECT command shows the Title and pub_name columns from the Titles and Publishers tables. The only rows that are displayed are those in which the contents of the pub_id column in both tables are the same. Therefore, a synchronization between the tables is created.

Chapter 9

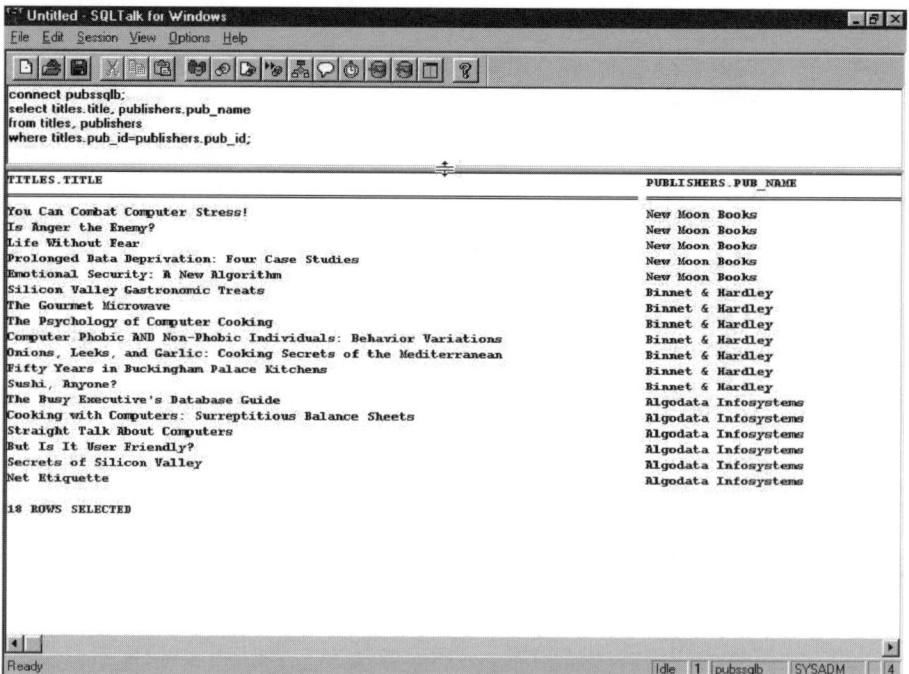

Calculations with Columns of Distinct Tables

The next example shows how to create a query that displays the results based on fields of columns from different tables. Consider this code:

```
SELECT * FROM sales;
SELECT s.title_id, s.qty, t.price, s.qty*t.price AS totsale, t.title
FROM sales s, titles t
WHERE s.title_id=t.title_id
ORDER BY t.title;
```

The Qty (Quantity) field of the Sales table is multiplied by the Price field of the Titles table for the records with the same title_id code.

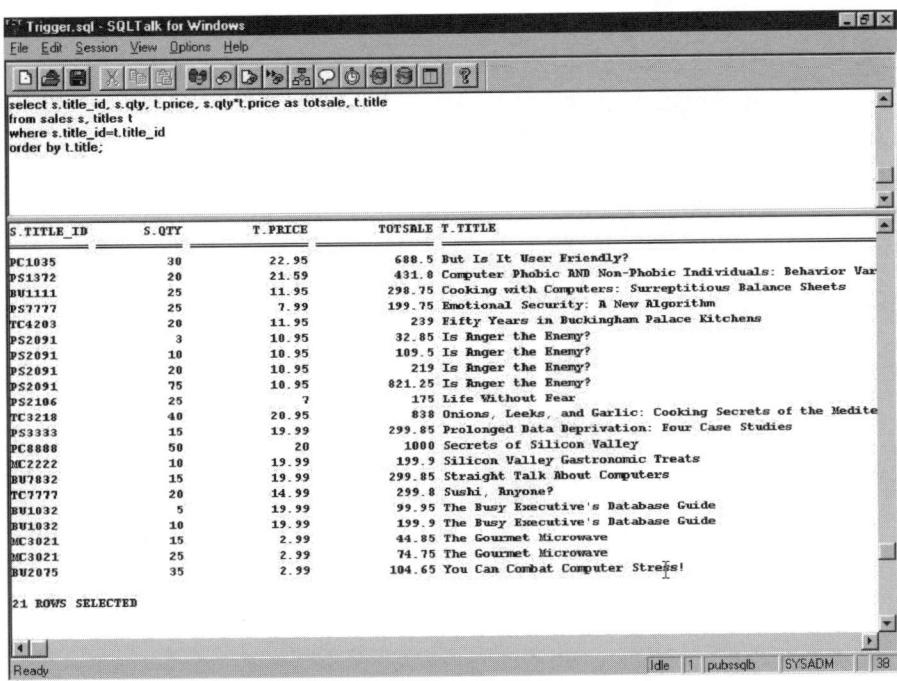

Here is another example where only those books that have total sales of five or more and have a code of PS are displayed.

Input:

SELECT s.title_id, s.qty, t.price, s.qty*t.price AS totsale, t.title
FROM sales s, titles t
WHERE s.qty >=5 AND s.title_id LIKE 'PS%' AND s.title_id=t.title_id
ORDER BY t.title;

Result:

S.TITLE_ID	S.QTY	T.PRICE	TOTSALE	T.TITLE
PS1372	20	21.59	431.8	Computer Phobic AND Non-Phobic
PS7777	25	7.99	199.75	Emotional Security: A New Algorithm
PS2091	10	10.95	109.5	Is Anger the Enemy?
PS2091	20	10.95	219	Is Anger the Enemy?
PS2091	75	10.95	821.25	Is Anger the Enemy?
PS2106	25	7	175	Life Without Fear
PS3333	5	19.99	299.85	Prolonged Data Deprivation: Four Case Studies

Joins Based on Non-Equality

Often we must create a join of tables that displays only those rows that satisfy conditions that do not apply to the rows of both tables. In the Pubssqlb database, the Roysched table stores a list of rows with the percentage of royalties to be paid to each author, depending on the number of books sold. We will show the partial contents of this table just for the books that have a code beginning with the letter P.

Input:

```
SELECT * FROM roysched
WHERE title_id LIKE 'P%';
```

This query shows the contents of the Roysched table, which contains the percentage of royalty to be paid to the authors. Each book has several ranges of royalty based on the number sold. Below is an example for the book PC1035.

From	up to	%
0	2000	10
2001	3000	12
3001	4000	14
4001	10000	16

To discover the Royalty value that must be paid we need to know the book's sales. The next query performs this task. It selects the code of the book, the number of annual sales, and the range of royalties. The WHERE clause initially synchronizes the rows with the same title code in both tables. Then it returns the row with the value of annual sales in the Titles table that is between the values of the lorange and hirange columns.

```
SELECT t.title_id, t.ytd_sales, r.royalty
FROM roysched r, titles t
WHERE t.title_id=r.title_id
AND t.ytd_sales >= r.lorange
AND t.ytd_sales <= r.hirange;
```

TITLE_ID	LORANGE	HIRANGE	ROYALTY
PC1035	0	2000	10
PC1035	2001	3000	12
PC1035	3001	4000	14
PC1035	4001	10000	16
PC1035	10001	50000	18
PS2091	0	1000	10
PS2091	1001	5000	12
PS2091	5001	10000	14
PS2091	10001	50000	16
PS2106	0	2000	10
PS2106	2001	5000	12
PS2106	5001	10000	14
PS2106	10001	50000	16
PC8888	0	5000	10
PC8888	5001	10000	12
PC8888	10001	15000	14
PC8888	15001	50000	16
PS7777	0	5000	10
PS7777	5001	50000	12
PS3333	0	5000	10
PS3333	5001	10000	12
PS3333	10001	15000	14
PS3333	15001	50000	16
PS1372	0	10000	10
PS1372	10001	20000	12
PS1372	20001	30000	14
PS1372	30001	40000	16
PS1372	40001	50000	18

28 ROWS SELECTED

T.TITLE_ID	T.YTD_SALES	R.ROYALTY
BU1032	4095	10
BU1111	3876	10
BU2075	18722	24
BU7832	4095	10
MC2222	2032	12
MC3021	22246	24
PC1035	8780	16
PC8888	4095	10
PS1372	375	10
PS2091	2045	12
PS2106	111	10
PS3333	4072	10
PS7777	3336	10
TC3218	375	10
TC4203	15096	14
TC7777	4095	10

16 ROWS SELECTED

Note that the book PC1035 has sold 8,780 books in the year, putting it in the 16% royalty range.

The Pubssqlb database has a Titleauthor table that is used to join all the authors and their books. When the database was created, this table was designed instead of putting the author code in the Titles tables. Following is a partial listing of this table, showing the author's code, title code, the

92 ■ Chapter 9

author's percentage of royalty (royaltyper), and an order number (the importance of the author).

AU_ID	TITLE_ID	ROYALTYPER	AU_ORD
213-46-8915	BU1032	40	2
409-56-7008	BU1032	60	1
267-41-2394	BU1111	40	2
724-80-9391	BU1111	60	1
213-46-8915	BU2075	100	1
274-80-9391	BU7832	100	1
712-45-1867	MC2222	100	1

If you check the contents of this table in Appendix F, you will see that there are 25 records. Since there are a total of 17 titles published, some of the books must have more than one author. When this happens, the royalty percentage can be different among the authors.

When you create a join with more than two tables, you do not necessarily need to return columns from all the tables. The next example returns the authors, their royalty percentage, and the title listed in title code order, which is not shown.

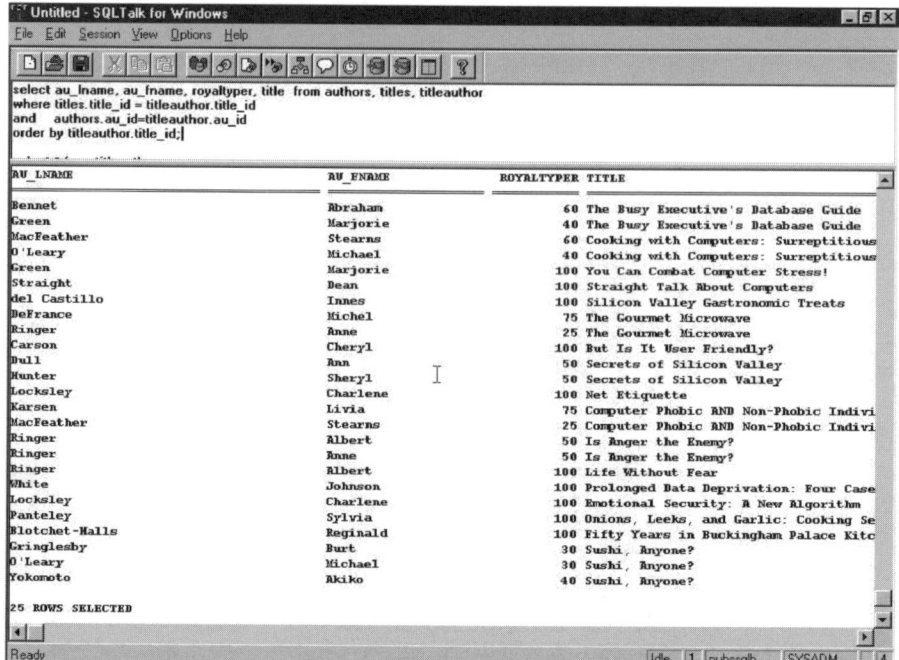

Combining the Results with UNION

While it does not cause a joining of tables, the UNION operator allows you to combine the result of two or more queries in one set of results. The sets returned by each SELECT command must have the same structure, i.e., they must specify the same columns.

The syntax of this operator is:

```
select_statement UNION [ALL] select_statement
```

Input:

```
CREATE TABLE dmov
(codprod char(4) not null,
nameprod char(20) not null,
cost int);

INSERT INTO dmov values ('005', 'eeee' ,10);
INSERT INTO dmov values ('006', 'ffff' ,80);
INSERT INTO dmov values ('007', 'gggg' ,70);

SELECT * FROM dmov;
SELECT * FROM test1;
```

Result:

CODPROD	NAMEPROD	COST
005	eeee	10
006	ffff	80
007	gggg	70

CODPROD	NAMEPROD	COST
001	aaaa	10
002	bbbb	40
003	cccc	30
004	dddd	20

Input:

```
SELECT * FROM test1
UNION
SELECT * FROM dmov;
```

Result:

```
CODPROD   NAMEPROD   COST
=======   ========   ====
001       aaaa       10
002       bbbb       40
003       cccc       30
004       dddd       20
005       eeee       10
006       ffff       80
007       gggg       70
```

The names of the columns displayed in the result are the names of the columns in the first SELECT command. In this example, the columns had the same names.

By default, the UNION operator removes duplicate rows from the result set. If you use ALL, all rows are included in the results and duplicates are not removed.

Consider the Test2 table, which has the following contents:

```
CODPROD   NAMEPROD   COST
=======   ========   ====
001       aaaa       10
002       bbbb       40
009       cccc       30
004       dddd       20
```

Note that it is identical in contents to the Test1 table, with the exception of the third row where the code is 009. Now see what happens when we execute the next group of commands:

```
SELECT * FROM test1
UNION
SELECT * FROM dmov
UNION
SELECT * FROM test2;
```

Instead of displaying all the rows of all three tables, just one row of the Test2 table is displayed: the one with code = 009. The remaining rows that are identical to the rows of the Test1 table are eliminated from the set of results.

```
CODPROD   NAMEPROD   COST
=======   ========   ====
001       aaaa       10
002       bbbb       40
003       cccc       30
004       dddd       20
005       eeee       10
006       ffff       80
007       gggg       70
009       cccc       30
```

When the UNION operator is used, the SELECT commands cannot individually use ORDER BY. (Only after the last SELECT can you use ORDER BY or COMPUTE, if the dialect allows you to do so.) On the other hand, GROUP BY and HAVING can only be used in individual SELECT commands.

Summary

In this chapter you have seen the principles used to create joins among two or more tables. This is probably one of the most powerful resources of SQL. In the next chapter we will discuss subqueries.

Review Questions

1. What are join tables?
2. What is an equi-join?
3. What is the purpose of the UNION clause?
4. Write a command that shows all the fields of three different tables at the same time.

Chapter 10
Subqueries

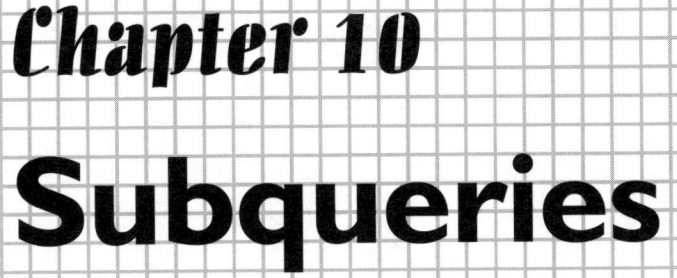

- Correlated subqueries
- The IN and NOT IN options
- The EXISTS operator
- Nested subqueries

A *subquery* is a query that has its results passed as arguments to another query. Through a subquery you can create complex queries, using the results of the subquery as a predicate of the query that contains it. There are several types of subqueries; the main types are correlated subqueries and non-correlated subqueries.

The basic syntax of a SELECT command that has a subquery is the following:

```
SELECT [DISTINCT] column_list
FROM table_list
WHERE
{ expression  { [NOT] IN comparison_operator  [ANY| ALL] }| [NOT]
EXISTS }

(SELECT [DISTINCT] column_list
FROM column_list
WHERE conditions)

[GROUP BY list]
[ORDER BY list]
[HAVING conditions]
```

A query is built inside parentheses in the WHERE clause of the main query, and its results are compared to some expression.

A subquery often performs exactly like a join, as shown in the following example:

Input:

```
SELECT DISTINCT pub_name FROM publishers p, titles t
WHERE p.pub_id=t.pub_id
AND type='psychology';
```

Result:

```
PUB_NAME
================
Binnet & Hardley
New Moon Books
```

Non-Correlated Query

A *non-correlated query* is a query that is independent of the previous query. Each one works with data from distinct tables without using the columns of the tables mentioned in the first query.

The previous example would resemble the following non-correlated subquery:

```
SELECT pub_name FROM publishers
WHERE pub_id IN
(SELECT pub_id FROM titles WHERE type='psychology');
```

In this case the subquery is non-correlated, since it is totally independent of the previous query. Note that the first SELECT command uses only the Publishers table. The subquery, which can also be called an inner query, works only with data from the Titles table.

Correlated Query

A *correlated* subquery uses data from the external query, as shown below:

```
SELECT pub_name FROM publishers p
WHERE 'psychology' IN
(SELECT type FROM titles WHERE pub_id=p.pub_id);
```

In this example the subquery compares the pub_id field of the Titles table, which is referenced in the subquery, with the field of the same name in the Publishers table, which is referenced by the external query.

A non-correlated query works from inside out, i.e., an external, or superior, query is executed only after the inner query is executed. The external query is executed based on the result of the inner query.

A correlated query works differently. The external query is partially executed, making available those columns or expressions that are used by the inner query. This, in turn, is executed using data from the external query that returns the result that is evaluated by the external query and closes its execution.

Values Returned by a Subquery

Depending on the way it is assembled, a subquery can return three types of values:

- A logical value that tests some existence through the use of the EXISTS predicate
- A unique value returned through the use of a comparison operator
- One or more values through the use of the IN predicate

In the initial examples, the subqueries returned more than one result value in the IN predicate. When a subquery uses comparison operators, it always returns only one value. When a subquery does not return any value, the result is considered to be false, although in practical terms an unknown value has been returned.

Restrictions on Subqueries

There are some limitations to the use of subqueries. Be sure to check whether the dialect your database uses has limitations of its own.

- A subquery cannot use the ORDER BY or INTO clauses inside the SELECT command of the subquery.
- The SELECT command of a subquery that starts with EXISTS normally uses * instead of a list of fields, since the subquery is testing whether rows that satisfy a condition of the WHERE clause exist. However, in most dialects there are no errors when you use it.
- The GROUP BY and HAVING clauses will work correctly only when they return a unique value in the subquery.
- The selection list of the subquery that is invoked by a comparison operator or IN predicate must contain only one expression or column name, as well as the expression used in WHERE that could possibly be related (joined) with the column in the selection list of the subquery.

Using the Aggregate Functions

Using the aggregate functions guarantees that a subquery will return only one value. For example, when you want to know what books are priced below the average price, you can use the following subquery:

Input:

```
SELECT AVG(price) FROM titles;
SELECT title_id, price FROM titles
WHERE
price < (SELECT AVG(price) FROM titles);
```

Result:

```
AVG(PRICE)
===========
14.76625

1 ROW SELECTED

TITLE_ID  PRICE
========  =====
BU1111    11.95
BU2075    2.99
MC3021    2.99
PS2091    10.95
PS2106    7
PS7777    7.99
TC4203    11.95

7 ROWS SELECTED
```

Only the rows for the books with prices below the average price (14.76625) in the table will be returned. The inner query finds the average value and the external query uses it to create your query.

Generally subqueries are invoked through a logical comparison operator or the IN and EXISTS predicates and are modified by ANY and ALL. We will see some examples throughout the rest of this chapter.

Using IN and NOT IN

The following is the syntax for using IN and NOT IN:

```
Expression [ IN | NOT IN] (SELECT selection_list WHERE expression
[NOT] IN (subquery)   )
```

We want to know which authors have 100% of the copyright, that is, how many authors share in the royalty. One of the options would be to query the Authors table to obtain the name of the author and use a subquery to check which authors receive 100% of the royalty.

Input:

```
SELECT * FROM titleauthor;
SELECT au_id, au_lname FROM authors
WHERE
au_id IN (SELECT au_id FROM titleauthor WHERE royaltyper=100);
```

Result:

AU_ID	AU_LNAME
===========	=============
172-32-1176	White
213-46-8915	Green
238-95-7766	Carson
274-80-9391	Straight
486-29-1786	Locksley
648-92-1872	Blotchet-Halls
712-45-1867	del Castillo
807-91-6654	Panteley
998-72-3567	Ringer

9 ROWS SELECTED

If you check the complete contents of the Titleauthor table in Appendix F, you will see that some authors hold 100% of the copyright of a book and others hold less since they are co-authors.

If you want to know how many copies of a particular book sold, you can use the following command:

```
SELECT SUM(qty) FROM sales WHERE title_id='PS2091';
```

The result is 108. Now, if you want to know the amount of sales inside and outside the state of California, you can use a subquery with the IN and NOT IN predicates, where the subquery selects the rows of the Store table that has a store code pertaining to California.

In this next example only the sales made by stores in California are returned.

Input:

```
SELECT title_id, qty, stor_id  FROM sales
WHERE title_id= 'PS2091'
AND stor_id  IN (SELECT stor_id FROM stores WHERE state='CA');
```

Result:

```
TITLE_ID  QTY  STOR_ID
========  ===  =======
PS2091    75   7066
PS2091    10   7067
```

To exclude the sales in California, simply add NOT to the same query, as shown below:

Input:

```
SELECT title_id, qty, stor_id FROM sales
WHERE title_id= 'PS2091'
AND stor_id NOT IN (SELECT stor_id FROM stores WHERE state='CA');
```

Result:

```
TITLE_ID  QTY  STOR_ID
========  ===  =======
PS2091    3    6380
PS2091    20   7131
```

Using EXISTS

EXISTS returns a value that may be true or false. It uses a subquery as an argument. After its evaluation it returns true when the subquery produces some result, i.e, when it returns a row. When no result is produced, it returns false.

This operator can be used with NOT, which inverts the result returned. In other words, EXISTS can be used to find the intersection of two tables or the differences between two tables.

Imagine that a publisher intends to organize an event to launch the book of each author in his or her own state. To do that, it needs to compare the State column of the Stores table with the State column of the Authors table. To see the authors who have stores in their states, we could use the EXISTS operator in a correlated subquery, such as in the next example. Just remember that the table only lists bookstores in three states: Washington, California, and Oregon.

Input:

```
SELECT au_lname, state FROM authors
WHERE
EXISTS (SELECT * FROM stores st
WHERE state= authors.state);
```

Result:

```
AU_LNAME              STATE
===============       =====
White                 CA
Green                 CA
Carson                CA
O'Leary               CA
Straight              CA
Bennet                CA
Dull                  CA
Gringlesby            CA
Locksley              CA
Yokomoto              CA
Stringer              CA
MacFeather            CA
Karsen                CA
Hunter                CA
McBadden              CA
Blotchet-Halls        OR

16 ROWS SELECTED
```

On the other hand, to find out which authors do not have bookstores in their state, simply add NOT.

Input:

```
SELECT au_lname, state FROM authors
WHERE
NOT EXISTS (SELECT * FROM stores st
WHERE state= authors.state);
```

Result:

```
AU_LNAME        STATE
============    =======
Smith           KS
Greene          TN
del Castillo    MI
```

```
DeFrance      IN
Panteley      MD
Ringer        UT
Ringer        UT
```

Nested Subqueries

Depending on the database design, a subquery may be the only way to obtain the desired result. The Pubssqlb database uses the Titleauthor table as a link between the authors and their books. To show how this relationship works, the next example uses a join to relate the tables and show the business books' authors:

```
SELECT a.au_lname, t.title_id FROM authors a, titles t, titleauthor
WHERE a.au_id= titleauthor.au_id
AND t.title_id= titleauthor.title_id
AND t.type='business';
```

Result:

```
A.AU_LNAME       T.TITLE_ID
==========       ==========
Green            BU1032
Bennet           BU1032
O'Leary          BU1111
MacFeather       BU1111
Green            BU2075
Straight         BU7832

6 ROWS SELECTED
```

Remember that some books have more than one author, as is the case of titles BU1032 and BU1111.

Let's try to understand this relationship:

SELECT a.au_lname, t.title_id FROM authors a, titles t, titleauthor	Selects the au_lname and title_id fields from the Authors and Titles tables.
WHERE a.au_id= titleauthor.au_id	Where the au_id field from the Authors table is identical to the au_id field of the Titleauthor table. Here, a relationship is established between the Authors and Titleauthor tables.

AND t.title_id= titleauthor.title_id	In which the title_id field of the Titleauthor table is identical to the title_id field of the Titles table. Here, a relationship is established through titles, i.e., the rows of the Authors table are synchronized with the rows of the Titles table. Each author found in the Authors table will have data about their books available.
AND t.type='business';	Just the rows containing books in the "business" category are returned from the Titles table.

If you want to know which authors have already sold books, access the Sales table, which shows the bookstores' orders and the number of books sold for each title. But this table has no author code. The only way to identify the author is by using the title_id column to relate it with the Titleauthor table, which in turn will be related through the au_id field with the Authors table.

The Sales table has 21 records (see Appendix F for the table's contents) showing the sale of 14 different titles; this means that more than one order was placed for some of the titles. We will use two subqueries to execute this task. First note the query and the rows returned:

Input:

```
SELECT au_lname, au_fname  FROM authors
WHERE au_id IN (SELECT au_id FROM titleauthor
WHERE title_id IN (SELECT title_id FROM sales));
```

Result:

```
AU_LNAME              AU_FNAME
================      ========
White                 Johnson
Green                 Marjorie
Carson                Cheryl
O'Leary               Michael
Straight              Dean
Bennet                Abraham
Dull                  Ann
Gringlesby            Burt
Locksley              Charlene
Blotchet-Halls        Reginald
Yokomoto              Akiko
del Castillo          Innes
DeFrance              Michel
```

```
MacFeather          Stearns
Karsen              Livia
Panteley            Sylvia
Hunter              Sheryl
Ringer              Anne
Ringer              Albert
```

19 ROWS SELECTED

Since some books have more than one author, 19 authors with sales were displayed.

Next is an analysis of this command:

SELECT au_lname, au_fname FROM authors	Selects the au_lname and au_fname fields of the Authors table
WHERE au_id IN (SELECT au_id FROM titleauthor	Where the au_id field (from the Authors table) appears in the result of the subquery (SELECT au_id FROM titleauthor)
WHERE title_id IN (SELECT title_id FROM sales)) ;	That in turn has the title_id field (from the Titleauthor table contained in the Sales table).

Actually, all 21 rows of sales will be queried but only 14 will be returned by the last subquery. Then, for each row returned a title_id code is found in the Titleauthor table, which in turn connects itself to the Authors table for the external query that is executed and that returns 19 records.

To find the average number of sales by book in the Sales table, use the following:

Input:

```
SELECT title_id, AVG(qty), SUM(qty), COUNT(qty) FROM sales
GROUP BY title_id;
```

Result:

```
TITLE_ID  AVG(QTY)  SUM(QTY)  COUNT(QTY)
========  ========  ========  ==========
BU1032    7.5       15        2
BU1111    25        25        1
BU2075    35        35        1
BU7832    15        15        1
MC2222    10        10        1
```

```
MC3021    20    40    2
PC1035    30    30    1
PC8888    50    50    1
PS1372    20    20    1
PS2091    27   108    4
PS2106    25    25    1
PS3333    15    15    1
PS7777    25    25    1
TC3218    40    40    1
TC4203    20    20    1
TC7777    20    20    1
```

Now let's locate the books with orders that are above the sales average for the title.

Input:

```
SELECT  title_id, qty  FROM sales
WHERE qty > (SELECT AVG(qty) FROM sales sb
WHERE sales.title_id=sb.title_id);
```

Result:

```
TITLE_ID  QTY
========  ===
BU1032    10
MC3021    25
PS2091    75
```

As a comparison, take a look at the following orders for the books. Notice that only the books with sales above the average were returned in the result above.

```
TITLE_ID  QTY  ORD_NUM
========  ===  ========
BU1032     5   6871
BU1032    10   423LL930
MC3021    15   423LL922
MC3021    25   N914014
PS2091     3   722a
PS2091    10   D4482
PS2091    20   N914008
PS2091    75   QA7442.3
```

Using ANY, ALL, and SOME

The SQL language offers some options that although redundant can be used to obtain a unique result when a subquery returns a group of rows.

The Employee table has 43 rows (see Appendix F for its contents). It contains details about the salary ranges of the available jobs (job_id). We will take a look at the salaries (job_lvl) in each range and the statistical data in the form of minimum, maximum, and average values for each job. For example, there are four employees who hold the job with code 10. Their salaries range from $75,000 to $165,000, with an average salary of $101,750.

Input:

```
SELECT job_id, AVG(job_lvl), MIN(job_lvl), MAX(job_lvl), COUNT(job_lvl)
FROM employee
GROUP BY job_id;
```

Result:

JOB_ID	AVG(JOB_LVL)	MIN(JOB_LVL)	MAX(JOB_LVL)	COUNT(JOB_LVL)
2	215	215	215	1
3	200	200	200	1
4	227	227	227	1
5	187.2857143	150	246	7
6	176	140	220	4
7	142.5	120	195	4
8	125.25	100	175	4
9	123.25	75	170	4
10	101.75	75	165	4
11	121.75	75	150	4
12	55.66666667	32	100	3
13	66.33333333	35	100	3
14	74.66666667	35	100	3

Now we will create a query using the modifier ALL to list all the employees who earn more than the employees in department 10. ALL returns the greater value returned by the subquery.

Input:

```
SELECT fname, job_lvl FROM employee
WHERE job_lvl >ALL
(SELECT job_lvl FROM employee WHERE job_id=10);
```

Result:

```
FNAME           JOB_LVL
=========       =======
Francisco       227
Philip          215
Ann             200
Carlos          211
Palle           195
Karla           170
Matti           220
Janine          172
Laurence        175
Rita            198
Maria           246
Diego           192
Mary            175
Gary            170

14 ROWS SELECTED
```

Note that only the jobs with a salary greater than $165,000 were returned.

The modifiers ANY and SOME return the smallest value of the group of rows in the subquery. In the next example, all the rows with a salary greater than any salary of the employees in department 10 will be returned. In other words, any salary greater than $75,000 will be returned, since that is the smallest salary in the department.

```
SELECT fname, job_lvl FROM employee
WHERE job_lvl > ANY
(SELECT job_lvl FROM employee WHERE job_id=10);

FNAME           JOB_LVL
=========       =======
Pedro           89
Victoria        140
Lesley          120
Francisco       227
Philip          215
Aria            87
Ann             200
Anabela         100
Paul            159
Carlos          211
```

```
Palle        195
Karla        170
Karin        100
Matti        220
Pirkko        80
Janine       172
Maria        135
Laurence     175
Patricia     150
Roland       150
Rita         198
Helvetius    120
Timothy      100
Sven         150
Miguel       112
Paula        125
Manuel       101
Maria        246
Diego        192
Annette      152
Mary         175
Margaret      78
Howard       100
MartÝn       165
Gary         170

35 ROWS SELECTED
```

Summary

This chapter introduced the concept of subqueries. You learned the basic types of queries (correlated and non-correlated) and the operators and modifiers that can be applied to subqueries. The next chapter discusses how to create tables and indexes.

Review Questions

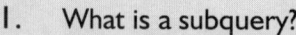

1. What is a subquery?
2. What is a correlated query?
3. What is a non-correlated query?
4. What is the purpose of the EXISTS clause?
5. What is the purpose of the IN clause?
6. What is the purpose of the ALL modifier?
7. What is the purpose of the ANY modifier?

Day 3

Chapter

11—Tables and Indexes

12—Maintaining Tables

13—Views

14—Embedded SQL

15—Miscellaneous

Chapter 11
Tables and Indexes

- Creating tables
- Referential integrity
- Creating indexes
- The UNIQUE clause

Tables are the heart of a database. Knowing how to create and maintain tables is very important for database users. This chapter also discusses indexes, which are database components used to speed up data access.

Tables

Before creating a table you should carefully define the database. Many developers have the bad habit of defining a database "on the fly," i.e., they open the module that creates the tables and then start thinking about how the database should look. This can cause many problems.

Each column must be created based on the specification of some basic information, such as name, type of data that it will store, and, optionally, the specification of any default values and constraints, or limitations.

The name of a column must be unique in a table. There cannot be two columns called "State" inside the same table. However, different tables inside the same database can contain columns with same name. For example, a Clients table and a Vendors table can both contain address data in columns called "Address," "City," and "State."

The name of the table must be unique among tables created by a particular owner; however, inside a database, there can be tables with the same name that belong to different users.

Data Types

To create a table, you need to provide information such as the name of the table, the name of the columns, and the type of data each column will store. Each column must have a data type specified to it. See Appendix C for a detailed description of types allowed in your database.

Below are the data types for SQLBase:

Table 11-1. SQLBase Data Types

Data Type	Description
Char	Character type data with fixed size of up to 254 characters.
Date	Stores only the date.
Datetime or Timestamp	When part of the entry argument is omitted, SQLBase assumes the default 0 that converts the date to 12/30/1899 and 12:00 a.m.

Table 11-1. SQLBase Data Types (continued)

Data Type	Description
Decimal or Dec	Supports up to 15 digits (-999999999999999 to +999999999999999). When this is not specified, a precision of 5 and scale of 0 is assumed.
Double precision	Type of numeric data code, floating-point with double precision.
Float	When the precision is specified between 1 and 21, the data type will have simple precision. Between 22 and 53, the precision is double.
Integer or Int	Integer type data with precision of up to 10 digits (-147483648 up to +2147483647).
Long Varchar	Stores characters or binary objects. This is equivalent to the data type blob.
Number	This is a super set of other data types. It supports precision of up to 22 digits.
Real	Numeric data type of floating-point and simple precision.
Time	Stores only the hour.
Smallint	This data type has no fractional digits. The digits to the right of the decimal point are truncated. It can have up to five digits of precision (-32768 to +32767).
Varchar	Character type data with fixed size of up to 254 characters.

Constraints

Many database vendors implement restrictions or constraints that limit the inclusion of data that does not satisfy certain conditions. Constraints are a way to guarantee the integrity of a database through the filtering of information inserted in a column. The constraints are the basic mechanism used to guarantee the integrity of a field. They have priority over triggers, rules, and default values. The main constraints are detailed below:

Not Null specifies that a column cannot accept the value null.

CHECK limits the values that can be put in a column by means of testing a Boolean condition based on the contents you intend to assign to the column. When the tested condition returns true, the value is assigned to the column.

UNIQUE forces the column to have unique values, i.e., a column cannot have two fields with the same contents. For example, a product code or social security number must be unique. However, the contents of a state or city column can appear in more than one row.

Primary Key creates the primary key of the table, i.e., a column or combination of columns containing values that must be unique inside the table in order to identify the row. A column that has a primary key constraint cannot have the Null value assigned to it. When the primary key is formed by more than a column, only one of them will be considered the primary key. The remaining columns that form the key are called *candidate keys*.

Foreign Key identifies the relationship among tables. This is a field in the current table that points to a key field in another table. This type of constraint prevents a value from being introduced in the current table that is not found in the key field of the foreign table that was joined. The use of a foreign key prevents the deletion of rows in the current table when there are references to key fields in other tables.

Null Values

Tables can have columns that do accept the value Null, which indicates that the column has not yet received any data. The columns must always be filled out, however, and may be created with an option that makes it mandatory for data to be supplied.

Primary Key

One or more columns of the table that exclusively identify a particular row inside the table form the *primary key*. The specification of a primary key guarantees the integrity of the table. The column or columns that form a primary key cannot contain the value null. When you specify a primary key, the database creates a specific index to guarantee that the primary key is unique.

In the example tables, the au_id and title_id columns are primary keys of the Authors and Books tables. The Titleauthor table has its primary key formed by the au_id and title_id columns. The primary keys are also used together to relate one table to the other.

Foreign Key

The *foreign key* is a column or combination of columns used to establish a link between two tables. The link is made by the creation of fields that are common to both tables. It is quite useful for keeping referential integrity between the two tables. For example, let's say you have an Employees table in which there is a Department field. This field is associated to the dep_id field in a Dept table that contains data from the company's departments. If there is no foreign key, anybody can delete a department's row from the Dept table when there are several employees with that department specified in their records. The foreign key allows only the insertion of values that can be found in the related fields of the foreign table.

While common, a foreign key does not necessarily have to be associated to the primary key in another table. However, it must reference a column which has unique contents.

The CREATE TABLE Command

The CREATE TABLE command is used to create a table and its columns. Each database has its own limitations on the number of columns and rows it can support. In SQLBase you can define a maximum of 253 columns for each table. To run this command, you must have RESOURCE, SYSADM, or DBA authority.

When you use CREATE TABLE with referential constraints, you can define a foreign key with the same specifications as the primary key in the parent table. You can also specify the rule of deletion for the referential constraint. The default rule is RESTRICT. The syntax in the following example applies to SQLBase.

Syntax:

```
CREATE TABLE table_name
(column_name data_type [NOT NULL] [NOT NULL WITH DEFAULT])
[PRIMARY KEY (column_name)]
[FOREIGN KEY [key_name] (column_name) REFERENCES parent_table_name
[ON DELETE [RESTRICT] [CASCADE] [SET NULL]]]
[IN [database_name] tablespace_name] [PCTFREE integer_constant]
[IN DATABASE database_name]
```

Arguments:

table_name
: A qualified table name has the form *identifier.table name*, where identifier is the name of the creator of the table.

data_type
: A column can contain one of the following data types:
    - Char (size)
    - Varchar (size)
    - Decimal [(precision, scale)]
    - Float
    - Integer
    - Long Varchar
    - Number
    - Smallint
    - Date
    - Datetime
    - Time
    - Timestamp

PRIMARY KEY
: Creates the primary key for the table. The following rules apply to the primary key:
    - If a table has a primary key, you must also create a unique index based on the columns of the key.
    - It cannot contain more than 16 columns; the sum of the attribute sizes of the columns cannot be greater than 255; it cannot contain columns with Long and Long Varchar data.
    - The values of the primary key must be unique.
    - A table can contain only one primary key.
    - The key can contain one or more columns.

FOREIGN KEY
: Specifies the foreign key for a table. Each value of the foreign key must contain a value corresponding to the original primary key.

Key name
: You can assign a name to the foreign key in order to identify it. This name can contain up to 18 characters. When this name is not provided, SQLBase creates a name based on the first column of the foreign key.

REFERENCES   Identifies the parent table in a relationship and defines the needed restrictions.

NOT NULL   Requires that data is contained in the column whenever a row is added to the table.

NOT NULL WITH DEFAULT
This clause prevents a column from containing null values and allows default values that are not null.

IN DATABASE database_name/IN [database_name] tablespace_name
SQLBase accepts these clauses but ignores them. They are compatible with DB2.

ON DELETE   Specifies the rules of deletion in a table. The default value is RESTRICT. These rules are used only to define a foreign key.

CASCADE   Deletes first the selected rows, then the dependent rows, ignoring the rules of deletion of the dependents.

RESTRICT   Specifies that the row can only be deleted when no other row depends on it.

SET NULL   Specifies that for every deletion performed in the primary key, the corresponding values in the foreign key are configured with null.

PCTFREE integer_constant
Configures the free space left in every row of the table when this is filled in for the first time. The default value is 10%. The value of PCTFREE must be between 0 and 99.

Variations

The CREATE TABLE command is the main command for the creation of a table. However, its syntax does vary a great deal from one dialect to another. Thus, we have included examples from Oracle and Microsoft SQL Server 7 using this command.

Oracle Examples

This example creates a table called Emp that is owned by user Scott. It uses the CONSTRAINT option to limit the contents of most columns. The analysis is shown after the command.

```
CREATE TABLE scott.emp
    (empno      NUMBER          CONSTRAINT pk_emp PRIMARY KEY,
     ename      VARCHAR2(10)    CONSTRAINT nn_ename NOT NULL
                                CONSTRAINT upper_ename
                                    CHECK (ename = UPPER(ename)),

     job        VARCHAR2(9),
     mgr        NUMBER          CONSTRAINT fk_mgr
                                    REFERENCES scott.emp(empno),

     hiredate   DATE            DEFAULT SYSDATE,
     sal        NUMBER(10,2)    CONSTRAINT ck_sal
                                    CHECK (sal > 500),

     comm       NUMBER(9,0)     DEFAULT NULL,
     deptno     NUMBER(2)       CONSTRAINT nn_deptno NOT NULL
                                CONSTRAINT fk_deptno
REFERENCES scott.dept(deptno) )
    PCTFREE 5 PCTUSED 75;
```

The Empno field is defined as the primary key. The Ename field only accepts text in uppercase, due to the CHECK constraint. The Mgr field checks the referential integrity with the Empno field in the Emp table. The Hiredate column accepts the date of the system as the default value. The Sal column only accepts values greater than 500.

The table definition adjusts the pctfree parameter to 5 and pctused to 75. The table also makes a reference to the integrity of its Deptno column to the Deptno column of the Dept table.

The next example creates a Scale table in the tablespace called HR, specifying the initial size of the table. The command also specifies that the table's index must be created in the area called user01.

```
CREATE TABLE scale
    ( grade    NUMBER    CONSTRAINT pk_salgrade
                         PRIMARY KEY
                         USING INDEX TABLESPACE user01

     losal    NUMBER,

     hisal    NUMBER )

    TABLESPACE HR

    STORAGE   (INITIAL        6144
               NEXT           6144
```

```
                        MINEXTENTS      1
                        MAXEXTENTS      5
                           PCTINCREASE  5);
```

Microsoft SQL Server 7 Examples

This example creates the Jobs table. The analysis is below the code.

```
CREATE TABLE jobs
(
job_id smallint
IDENTITY(1,1)
PRIMARY KEY CLUSTERED,
job_desc varchar(50) NOT NULL
DEFAULT 'not yet defined',
min_lvl tinyint NOT NULL
CHECK (min_lvl >= 10),
max_lvl tinyint NOT NULL
CHECK (max_lvl <= 250)
);
```

In this example, the job_id field is used as the primary key and uses one clustered index. The job_desc field does not accept nulls and has as its default value the text "not yet defined." The min_lvl field is of type tinyint; it does not accept nulls and only accepts values equal to or greater than 10. The max_lvl field also is of type tinyint. It does not accept nulls and only accepts values equal to or less than 250.

The following example creates the Employee table.

```
CREATE TABLE employee
(
emp_id empid
CONSTRAINT PK_emp_id PRIMARY KEY NONCLUSTERED
fname varchar(20) NOT NULL,
minit char(1) NULL,
lname varchar(30) NOT NULL,
job_id smallint NOT NULL   DEFAULT 1 REFERENCES jobs(job_id),
job_lvl tinyint DEFAULT 10,
pub_id char(4) NOT NULL DEFAULT ('9952') REFERENCES publishers(pub_id),
hire_date datetime NOT NULL DEFAULT (getdate())
```

This example uses a foreign key constraint to reference the job_id field in the Jobs table. In other words, it checks to see if the data that will be assigned to the job_id field of the Employee table exists in the Jobs table. The job_lvl, pub_id, and hire_date fields have default values automatically assigned to them when data is not entered using the INSERT or UPDATE commands.

Referential Integrity

Keeping the integrity of a database is one of the most important tasks in designing a database. When a field in a table must be present in a field in another table, we say that the field of the first table references the field in the second table. For example, in an Employees table there is a Dept column in which the department code must be provided. The database has another table called Tabdept that contains the code, name, and other information about the departments. When you insert an employee record, the department code must be included; otherwise the table will not be complete. The ideal situation would be to check and see if the data in the Dept column of the Employees table exists in the Tabdept table.

The field of the Employees table that references the field of the Tabdept table is called the foreign key, and the field that is referenced by it is called the *parent key*.

The names of the two fields do not need to be the same, but the data type must be identical. However, it is standard to use the same name to make it easier to see the relationship. A foreign key can reference parent keys formed by more than one column. For example, two letters and three numbers form a code. The two letters can be from a State field and the three numbers from a Codcity field, which contains a code signifying the city.

The referential integrity of the tables can be made during the creation of the table through the specification of the fields that have foreign keys, i.e., they are key fields in other tables. To create this control you must use the foreign key constraint. The implementations of these constraints vary from one database to the other as shown below:

In Oracle:
```
mgr NUMBER CONSTRAINT fk_mgr REFERENCES emp(empno),
```

In SQL Server 7:
```
job_id REFERENCES jobs(job_id)
```

In these two implementations the REFERENCES clause specifies the table and the parent key inside parentheses.

Below is the procedure for using foreign keys in SQLBase:

1. Create a table that has the foreign key used as primary key.
2. Create a table that contains a column used as foreign key and that references the table created in step 1.

In this example we will create two tables. One is called Typetab and contains the code and description of an item. It also contains the field with the primary key that will be referenced by the second table. After specifying the characteristics of both columns, the CREATE TABLE command indicates that the type_id field is the primary key. After the table is created, SQLBase requires that you create an index that uses the primary key. After creating the table and index we will insert four records in this table.

Input:

```
CREATE TABLE typetab
(
type_id char(3) NOT NULL,
type_desc char(20),
PRIMARY KEY (type_id)
);

CREATE UNIQUE INDEX type_IDX ON typetab(type_id);

INSERT INTO typetab values('001','Prod 01');
INSERT INTO typetab values('002','Prod 02');
INSERT INTO typetab values('003','Prod 03');
INSERT INTO typetab values('004','Prod 04');
SELECT * FROM typetab;
```

Result:

```
TYPE_ID   TYPE_DESC
=======   =========
001       Prod 01
002       Prod 02
003       Prod 03
004       Prod 04

4 ROWS SELECTED
```

Now we will create the Test4 table that references the type_id field of another table. After specifying the characteristics of the columns, the

CREATE TABLE command specifies that the column type is a foreign key and references the Typetab table.

```
CREATE TABLE test4
(cod char(4) NOT NULL,
 name char(20) NOT NULL,
 type char(3) NOT NULL,
 price int,
 FOREIGN KEY (type) references typetab);
```

Now let's insert two rows in the Test4 table.

Input:

```
INSERT INTO test4 values('A023','desc.01','002',200);
INSERT INTO test4 values('A024','desc.02','005',300);
```

Result:

```
1 ROW INSERTED
INSERT INTO test4 values('A023','desc.02','005',300)
                                           ^
Error: Unmatched foreign key values
```

The first row was inserted without any problems, because the code 002 assigned to the type_id field corresponds to the Typetab table. The second row that we tried to insert returns an error message saying that the foreign key was not located for the contents "005". If the value 005 is changed to 003, the row will be inserted normally.

Now let's insert some more rows. Note that the foreign key field can have the same value for different rows.

```
INSERT INTO test4 values('A024','desc.02','003',300);
INSERT INTO test4 values('A025','desc.03','004',400);
INSERT INTO test4 values('A026','desc.04','002',200);
INSERT INTO test4 values('A027','desc.05','003',300);
INSERT INTO test4 values('A015','desc.06','004',400);
INSERT INTO test4 values('A029','desc.07','002',200);
```

Using the foreign key is a way to reduce the risk of having a table that is incomplete. However, this does not prevent an incorrect code from being inserted in a table's field when it also exists in the referenced table.

The DROP TABLE Command

To remove a table from the database, you must use the DROP TABLE command. This command physically removes the table from inside the database, eliminating its data structure.

Syntax:

```
DROP TABLE table_name
```

The next example removes the Demo1 table from the current database:

```
DROP TABLE demo1
```

To remove a table that is in another database, you must specify the name of the database and use the .dbo extension.

```
DROP TABLE pubs.dbo.demo2
```

Indexes

Indexes are database components that speed up the access to data. They function similarly to a book's index, where instead of skimming the pages of the book to find where a particular subject is discussed, you check the index and locate the desired subject and its page number. Without an index, the search for a certain record takes much longer, since the records are simply stored in the order of creation.

In the case of a database, an index can be associated to a specific column or a combination of columns. You can also create several indexes for a table. Once the index is created, all the changes made to the table are automatically reflected in the index.

In the figure on the following page the Employees table has an index based on the emp_id column.

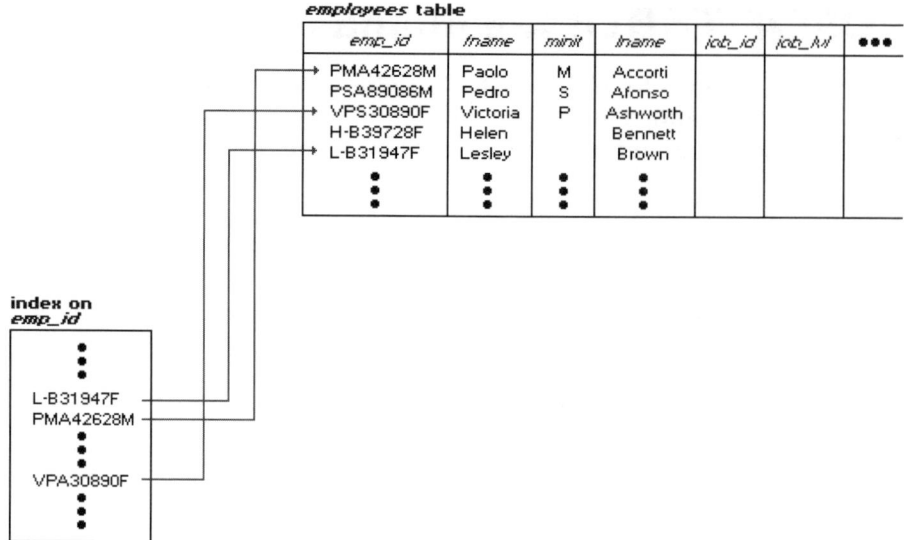

Indexes are very useful. There are some situations that must be considered, however, before the developer creates an index.

The data in a column normally indicates if an index must be created for it. Columns containing many rows with null values are not good candidates for indexing, nor are columns that have many identical values. Tables with a small number of rows are also not candidates. But columns that are used as primary keys must be indexed.

A table can contain a limited number of indexes. However, the greater the number, the greater the effort needed to manage and maintain the indexes, which can cause a decrease in performance, particularly in update or insert operations, since the database must update all the indexes.

An index can be created using the contents of one or more columns of the database. When more than one column is used, we say that the index is *compound*. The number of columns that can be used in a compound index depends on the database. When defining a compound index, the most important columns have precedence over the others.

The indexes can be of the unique type or non-unique type. Indexes of the unique type do not allow two rows in a table to have the same value.

The CREATE INDEX Command

The CREATE INDEX command is used to create indexes. It allows the creation of simple indexes, which use only one column, or compound indexes, which use more than one column. Here is the basic syntax of this command:

```
CREATE [UNIQUE] INDEX name ON schema.table ( column_name ASC/DESC ,...)
```

and an example:

```
CREATE INDEX indype ON test4(type);
```

Depending on the database, indexing may not cause a logical reorganization of the rows of a table when they are queried. To display the contents of a table in a certain order, you must use the SELECT command's ORDER BY clause.

Input:

```
SELECT * FROM test4;
```

Result:

```
CODE    NAME       TYPE    PRICE
====    =======    ====    =====
A023    desc.01    002     200
A024    desc.02    003     300
A025    desc.03    004     400
A026    desc.04    002     200
A027    desc.05    003     300
A015    desc.06    004     400
A029    desc.07    002     200
```

In this example, you should use the SELECT command with ORDER BY and order by type so the result is organized correctly.

Some database systems, such as SQL Server, use clustered indexes, which physically reorganize the rows of a table. In other words, the logical order is the same as the physical order of the rows.

The UNIQUE Clause

By creating an index with the UNIQUE clause we can force the integrity of the table, thus keeping two rows of the table from having the same contents for the key field. Consider the next example in which we create an index with the UNIQUE clause and then try to insert a new row that has the same contents as an already existing row.

Input:

```
CREATE UNIQUE INDEX  inddesc on test4(name);
INSERT INTO test4 values('A027','desc.05','003',300);
```

Result:

```
Error: Insert/update of unique constrained columns with duplicate data
```

A message warns that the data is duplicated in the column used as the key.

The DROP INDEX Command

An index should be maintained only when it is used effectively. Keeping an index that is not frequently used imposes a load on the system performance and occupies unnecessary disk space. Simply creating an index for a column does not necessarily mean that there will be any gain in performance, since it is a combination of several factors. If you detect through tests that there is no real gain in performance with an index, remove it. Periodically, an index can become very fragmented. In this case it's best to delete it and re-create it. The SQL command responsible for deleting an index is DROP INDEX.

Syntax:

```
DROP INDEX name
```

Example:

```
DROP INDEX depemp
```

Summary

In this chapter you have seen how to create and use tables and indexes, and also learned how to restrict the contents assigned to a column with constraints. You also learned about the foreign key and parent key, which implement referential integrity among tables. In the next chapter we will discuss the commands that maintain tables and other database objects.

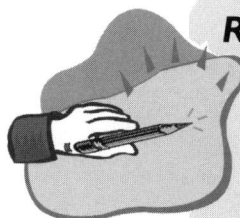

Review Questions

1. What are constraints?
2. What is the purpose of the CHECK constraint?
3. What is the purpose of the UNIQUE constraint?
4. What is the purpose of the NOT NULL constraint?
5. What is the purpose of the primary key constraint?
6. What is the purpose of the foreign key constraint?
7. What is referential integrity?
8. What is an index?
9. What command is used to create a table?
10. What command is used to delete a table?

Chapter 12
Maintaining Tables

- The INSERT command
- The DELETE command
- The UPDATE command
- The ALTER TABLE command

In the previous chapter you learned in detail how to create tables and indexes. Here, you learn how to add data to tables, make changes, and delete records. The commands responsible for these operations are INSERT, UPDATE, and DELETE.

These commands act similarly in both tables and views, a topic that we will discuss in the next chapter.

The INSERT Command

The INSERT command inserts a new row in the table and fills the columns with specific values. It is not necessary to assign contents to all the fields.

Basic syntax:

```
INSERT [INTO] {<table>} { { [(column_list)] VALUES
( {DEFAULT | constant_expression }[,...n]     )
```

Arguments:

- INTO — Indicates the name of the table that will receive data.
- column_list — This is a list of columns that will receive data. They must appear inside parentheses and be separated by commas. When the values specified in VALUES are not in the same order as the columns, the column_list option must be used to specify which columns will receive the values.
- VALUES — Specifies the list of values that will be inserted.
- DEFAULT — Assigns the default value to the column. When a default value is not defined, it is assigned as null.
- constant_expression
    This is a literal value, expression, or variable.

Recall one of the examples of INSERT that we saw in the first chapters of this book. Initially we created a table called Demo2. Then we inserted four records in the table. Note that the third record inserted had only the contents of two fields attributed. For this reason it was necessary to specify the names of the fields that would receive the specified values.

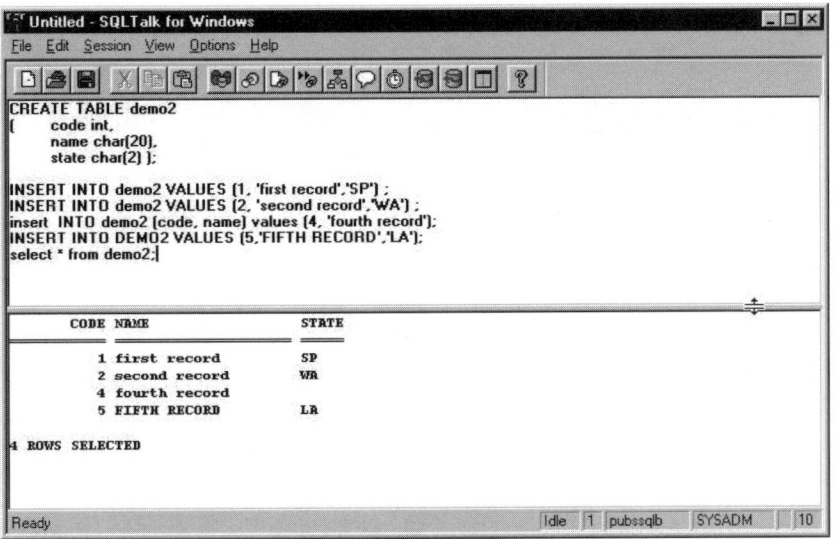

 **Note** While the basic syntax of a SQL declaration is the same, different databases may interpret it differently. Some require a particular clause while others consider it optional. Microsoft's SQL Server 7 accepts the use of the INSERT command with or without the INTO clause, while Oracle and SQLBase require the INTO clause. The contents of the fields must be specified inside single quotes in SQLBase, while SQL Server 7 uses double quotes. These differences can make life difficult for programmers who work with several different databases.

The specification order of the contents of fields must be the same as that used when the table was created. When you attribute contents to all the fields, there is no need to specify the list of columns. The command assumes that the first value goes in the first column, the second value in the second column, and so on.

Inserting Data in Specific Columns

When a table is created with the assignment of a default value for a column, the value is automatically inserted even if its contents are not specified in the INSERT command. When a column that was created with the NOT NULL constraint has no contents, this generates an error message and the record will not be included. The next figure shows the creation of a table in Oracle 8 in which one column has a default value and another is NOT NULL.

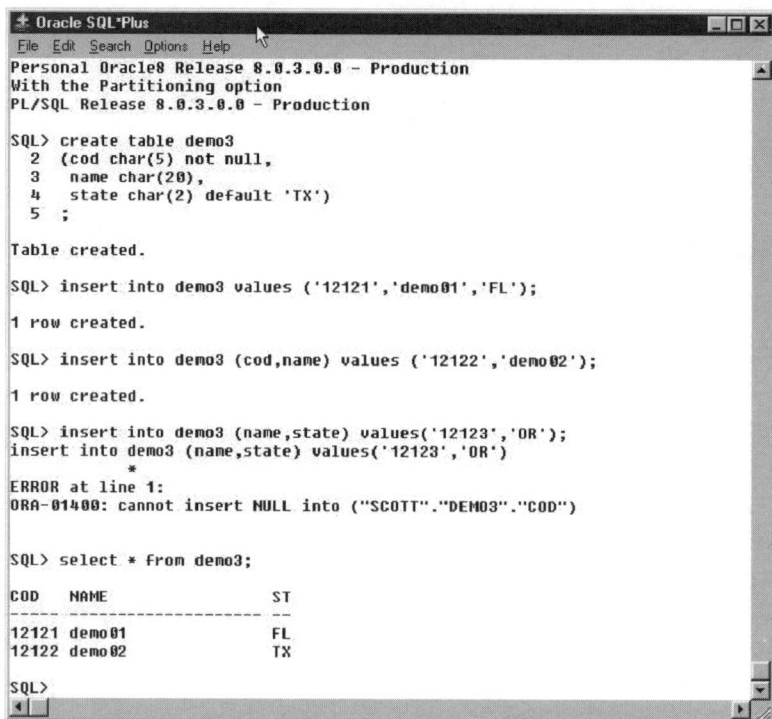

After inserting the first row with contents for all fields, we insert a second row omitting the State field, which has its contents automatically filled out. In the third example we omit the Cod field and an error message is generated.

In the example on the following page, also in Oracle 8, note that a new row is inserted with only a value in the Cod field.

Input:

SQL> INSERT INTO demo3 (cod) values ('12123');

1 row created.

SQL> SELECT * FROM demo3;

COD	NAME	ST
=====	======	==
12121	demo01	FL
12122	demo02	TX
12123		TX

```
SQL> SELECT * FROM demo3 WHERE name NOT LIKE '3%';

COD     NAME    ST
=====   ======  ==
12121   demo01  FL
12122   demo02  TX

SQL> SELECT count(name) FROM demo3;

COUNT(NAME)
===========
2

SQL> SELECT count(state) FROM demo3;

COUNT(STATE)
============
3
```

When a field has no value attributed to it, the database assigns the null value in case there is no default value associated to it. You can see that although there are three rows in the table, the operations involving the Name field do not consider the last row. Note that the COUNT function returns 2 when applied to the Name column and returns 3 when applied to the State column.

Inserting Data from Other Tables with SELECT

One of the most useful features of the INSERT command is the ability to insert rows from other tables into the target table of the insert. For example, a system can use one table for the daily tracking of sales, which is used to update the "official" Sales table after the daily closing.

The syntax of the INSERT command in this situation is:

```
INSERT [INTO] {<table>} { { [(column_list)] VALUES
SELECT column_list

FROM table

WHERE condition
```

The next example illustrates this technique. We will create a table called Demo5, insert four records in the table, and then create a table called Temp to show how to use the INSERT and SELECT commands.

Input:

```
CREATE TABLE demo5
(cod char(4),
 name char(15),
 cost int);
INSERT INTO demo5 values ('1111','Aaaaaaa',10);
INSERT INTO demo5 values ('2222','Bbbbbbb',20);
INSERT INTO demo5 values ('3333','Ccccccc',30);
INSERT INTO demo5 values ('4444','Dddddd',40);
SELECT * FROM demo5;
```

Result:

COD	NAME	COST
1111	Aaaaaaa	10
4444	Dddddd	40
2222	Bbbbbbb	20
3333	Ccccccc	30

The Temp table is created with the same structure for simplicity. A real table could have more or fewer fields (see "Inserting Specific Columns from Other Tables" later in this section). After creating the table we will insert a row using the regular INSERT command and then some lines from the Demo5 table.

Insert:

```
CREATE TABLE temp
(cod char(4),
 name char(15),
 cost int);

INSERT INTO temp values ('8888', 'Hhhhhh',80);

INSERT INTO temp
SELECT * FROM demo5
WHERE cod='4444';

INSERT INTO temp (cod, name)
SELECT cod, name FROM demo5
WHERE cod= '1111';
SELECT * FROM temp;
```

```
COD     NAME     COST
====    =======  ====
8888    Hhhhhh   80
4444    Dddddd   40
1111    Aaaaaaa
```

Using Expressions

SELECT lets the table receive data from allowed expressions in the SELECT command in order to update the target table. In the next example, the Temp table's Cost column is updated with the contents of the Demo5 table's Cost column multiplied by 1.5.

Input:

```
INSERT INTO temp
SELECT cod, name, cost*1.5 FROM demo5
WHERE cod= '2222';
SELECT * FROM temp;
```

Result:

```
COD     NAME     COST
====    =======  ====
8888    Hhhhhh   80
4444    Dddddd   40
1111    Aaaaaaa
2222    Bbbbbbb  30
```

Inserting Specific Columns from Other Tables

Often you need to insert a few columns from one table into another. The order of the columns may not be the same in both tables, although the contents of the columns are of the same type. In both cases, you can use the list of columns in the INSERT and SELECT commands to specify the order and the columns that will be inserted.

```
INSERT INTO temp (cod, name)
SELECT cod, name FROM demo5
WHERE cod= '1111';
SELECT * FROM temp;
```

```
COD     NAME       COST
====    =======    ====
8888    Hhhhhh     80
4444    Ddddd      40
1111    Aaaaaaa
```

The DELETE Command

The DELETE command removes from a table or view the rows that satisfy a specified condition. To delete a row, you simply specify the table where the row or set of rows that satisfy the condition are located.

Basic syntax:

```
DELETE FROM table_name [WHERE condition]
```

All the lines that are selected by the WHERE clause will be deleted.

Note Be very careful when using the DELETE command. If a particular row is not specified, every row in the table will be deleted.

Note in the following example the use of the WHERE clause to delete a row we added to the Temp table.

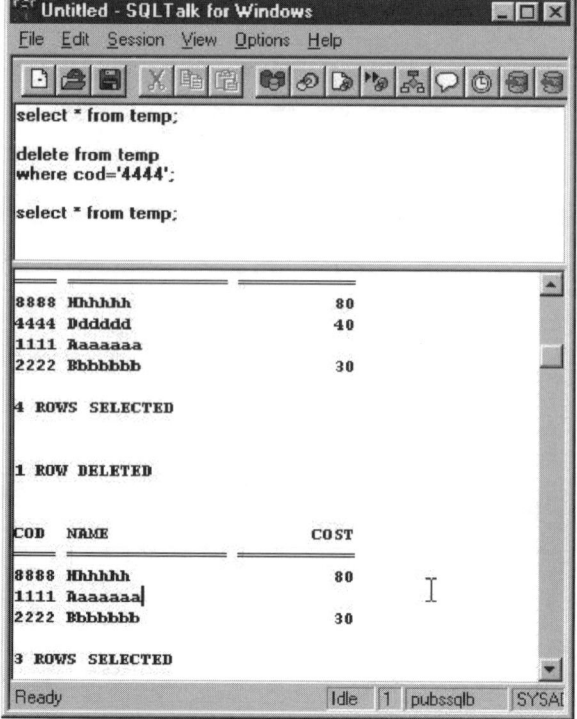

Deleting Rows from Tables with the Foreign Key

When you delete rows from a table, you can also create integrity problems for the database. For example, if a table has a foreign key that references another table and the row of the other table is deleted, there may be some problems. Some databases allow you to specify with the CREATE TABLE command what actions should be taken when rows are deleted.

SQLBase offers the ON DELETE option, which has similar counterparts in most other databases. ON DELETE specifies the rules to delete rows from the table. The default is RESTRICT, meaning only in the current table. The rules are used only in foreign key fields.

The next example creates two tables with referential integrity. The Emp table maintains general data on the employee, while the Empsal table maintains salary data. Empsal is created with the option ON DELETE CASCADE, indicating that if any row of the Emp table is deleted, the related rows in Empsal will also be automatically deleted in cascade.

```
CREATE TABLE emp
(empno INT NOT NULL,
 LNAME VARCHAR(15),
 FNAME CHAR(10),

 deptno SMALLINT,

 hiredate DATE,
 job VARCHAR (15),
 PRIMARY KEY (empno));

CREATE UNIQUE INDEX emp_idx ON emp (empno);

CREATE TABLE empsal
 (empno INTEGER,
salary DECIMAL (9,2),
 review LONG VARCHAR,
 FOREIGN KEY (empno) REFERENCES emp
 ON DELETE CASCADE);
```

After creating both tables we will enter some data:

```
INSERT INTO emp values (111, 'Ramalho', 'Jose', 2, '10/10/90',
'Writer');
INSERT INTO emp values (222, 'Hill', 'Jim', 2, '11/10/91', 'Manager');
INSERT INTO emp values (333, 'Muzilli', 'Marco', 1, '09/10/94',
'Physician');

INSERT INTO empsal (empno, salary) values(111,5000);
```

```
INSERT INTO empsal (empno, salary) values(222,6600);
INSERT INTO empsal (empno, salary) values(333,8000);
```

Note the contents of the tables:

```
SELECT * FROM emp;
SELECT * FROM empsal;
```

EMPNO	LNAME	FNAME	DEPTNO	HIREDATE	JOB
111	Ramalho	Jose	2	10-OCT-1990	Writer
222	Hill	Jim	2	10-NOV-1991	Manager
333	Muzilli	Marco	1	10-SEP-1994	Physician

3 ROWS SELECTED

EMPNO	SALARY	REVIEW
111	5000	
222	6600	
333	8000	

Now delete the record for the 222 code in the Emp table and check what happened:

Input:

```
DELETE FROM emp WHERE empno=222;

SELECT * FROM empsal;
SELECT * FROM emp;
```

Result:

2 rows deleted

EMPNO	LNAME	FNAME	DEPTNO	HIREDATE	JOB
111	Ramalho	Jose	2	10-OCT-1990	Writer
333	Muzilli	Marco	1	10-SEP-1994	Physician

EMPNO	SALARY	REVIEW
111	5000	
333	8000	

Both rows with the 222 code in the Emp and Empsal tables were deleted. You can use one subquery in the WHERE clause to delete data from the current table, based on the result of the subquery.

In a sales system you could delete from one table all the salespeople who sold less than 100,000 units. This piece of information should be queried in a second table that contains the sale orders.

The UPDATE Command

The UPDATE command allows you to update one or more fields of a row or group of rows in a table or view. The contents of each field must be adjusted with the SET clause. When more than one column is updated, the column=value pairs must be separated by commas.

Basic syntax:

```
UPDATE {<table_or_view>}
SET {column_name = {expression | DEFAULT} |
 [FROM { <table> | (select_statement) [AS] table_alias
 [ (column_alias [,…m]) ] |
 [WHERE <search_conditions>
```

Arguments:

SET	Specifies the list of columns that will be updated.
column_name	This is the name of the column to be updated. When it refers to a table other than the current one, it must be preceded by the name of the table or database.
expression	The new contents of the column; can be the result of a subselect that returns only one value.
DEFAULT	Indicates that the current contents must be replaced with the default value previously defined when the table was created.
FROM	Specifies that another table will be used to provide the update criteria for the operation.
WHERE	Specifies the conditions that must be satisfied to limit the number of rows that will be updated. When it is not specified, all the table's rows are updated.

Examine the next example, in which the contents of the Salary field for all the rows is increased by 1.1:

Input:

```
UPDATE empsal
SET salary=salary*1.1;
SELECT * FROM empsal;
```

Result:

EMPNO	SALARY
111	5500
333	8800

In the next example we use the WHERE clause to filter the changes. We will change the contents of the Salary field in the record that has a value greater than 6000.

Input:

```
UPDATE empsal
SET salary=salary*1.1
WHERE salary >6000;
SELECT * FROM empsal;
```

Result:

EMPNO	SALARY
111	5500
333	9680

The ALTER TABLE Command

Once a table is created, the SQL language allows you to change some of its characteristics.

This command can be used to add, delete, or change a column or to rename a column or table. The views that reference deleted or renamed columns or tables are automatically deleted. The precompiled commands that reference deleted or renamed columns or tables are not deleted.

Syntax:

```
ALTER TABLE table_name
DROP column_name
ADD column_name data_type [( size)] [NOT NULL] [NOT NULL WITH DEFAULT]
RENAME column_name new_name
         table_new_name
MODIFY column_name data_type ( length) [NULL]
                                       [NOT NULL]
                                       [NOT NULL WITH DEFAULT]
```

Arguments:

DROP — Removes a column from a table. If the column contains data, it is lost. You cannot delete an indexed column, a column that belongs to a key, or columns from the system catalog.

ADD — Adds a column to a table. The columns are created similarly to the CREATE TABLE command. ADD is the default clause if no clause is specified.

RENAME — Changes the name of a table or column. Tables and columns that are part of the system catalog cannot be renamed.

MODIFY — Changes a column's attributes. You can increase the size of a character column, but cannot decrease it. You also cannot change the column's data type or change the size of a numeric column.

NULL — Removes a column's NOT NULL attribute.

NOT NULL — Adds the NOT NULL attribute to columns that currently accept nulls. If the column contains null values, you cannot redefine it as NOT NULL.

NOT NULL WITH DEFAULT
    This clause prevents a column from containing null values and allows default values that are not null.

The next example changes the size of the Job column from 15 to 40 and makes it NOT NULL.

```
ALTER TABLE emp MODIFY job VARCHAR(40) NOT NULL;
```

Delete the Hiredate column:

```
ALTER TABLE emp DROP hiredate;
```

Now look at the results:

```
EMPNO   LNAME    FNAME   DEPTNO   JOB
=====   =======  =====   ======   =========
111     Ramalho  Jose    2        Writer
333     Muzilli  Marco   1        Physician
```

The next example changes the name of the Emp table to empxx1:

```
ALTER TABLE emp RENAME TABLE empxx1;
```

This command adds the attribute NOT NULL to the Job column:

```
ALTER TABLE empxx1 MODIFY job NOT NULL;
```

The following removes the attribute NOT NULL created in the last example:

```
ALTER TABLE empxx1 MODIFY job NULL;
```

Summary

This chapter explained in more detail how to insert, delete, and update the rows of a table by using the INSERT, DELETE, and UPDATE commands. You also saw how to change the characteristics of a table with the ALTER TABLE command. In the next chapter we will discuss how to create and use views.

Review Questions

1. What is the purpose of the INSERT command?
2. Write the basic syntax of the INSERT command.
3. What is the purpose of the DELETE command?
4. Write the basic syntax of the DELETE command.
5. What is the purpose of the UPDATE command?
6. Write the basic syntax of the UPDATE command.
7. What is the purpose of the ALTER TABLE command?

Chapter 13
Views

- Creating views
- Querying views
- Changing data with views

A *view* is a virtual table that has its contents defined by a database query. A view is not a physical table, but rather a set of instructions that returns a set of data. A view can be formed by columns from one or more tables. The following figure shows two tables that are the basis for the creation of a view.

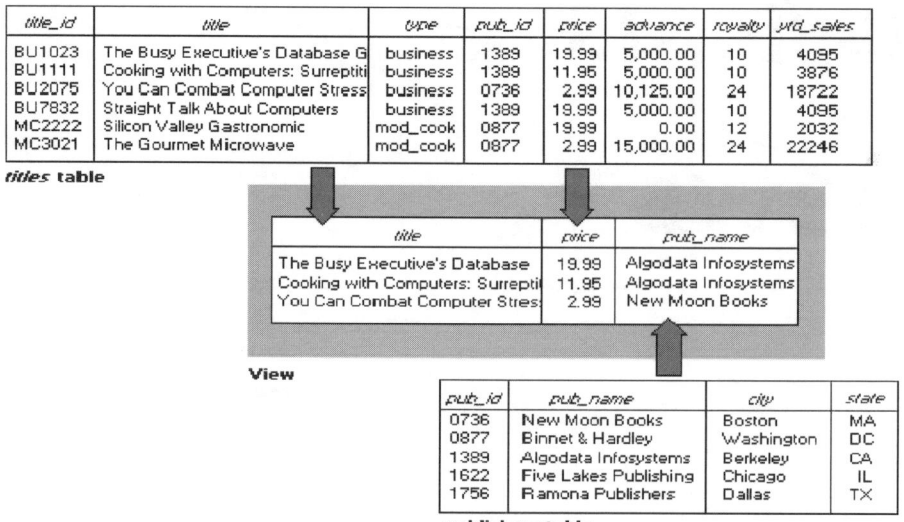

Views are particularly useful when you want to focus on certain types of information maintained by the database. Imagine a corporate database that is accessed by users in several departments. The information that the sales team manipulates is different from the data used by the billing or marketing departments. With views you can give the user just the information he or she needs, whether it comes from one or several tables of the database.

Views allow different users to see the same information from different perspectives. Views also allow information to be combined to satisfy certain criteria or even to be exported to other applications.

The definition of the table is internally stored in the data dictionary of the database. Another table is not physically created. The data viewed actually is the data in the tables that are the basis for creating the view. When data in a view is changed, the data in the original table changes. However, there are some limitations to these changes.

Advantages to Using Views

One of the biggest advantages of creating a view is that it makes querying the database easier for those users who only need certain information. This decreases the size and complexity of the SELECT commands.

Security is also an advantage of using views, since this prevents users from accessing data from a table that might be confidential. Although databases allow you to restrict access to certain tables, all the columns of the tables are available. In this case, you can create a view containing only those columns that pertain to that user.

Creating a View

Views are created with the CREATE VIEW command.

You can only modify tables using a view when it references only one table in the SELECT command's FROM clause, and the columns of the view are not derived from functions or arithmetic expressions. Also, you cannot use the ORDER BY clause in a view definition.

To create a view, you must have the SELECT privilege in the columns of the tables that form the view.

Syntax:

```
CREATE VIEW view_name [( column_name )]
AS SELECT [WITH CHECK OPTION]
```

Arguments:

view_name   The name of the view must follow this syntax: owner identifier.view name.

column_name
        Specifies names of columns, and must only be specified when you want the view's columns to have names different from the table's columns.

SELECT   A SELECT command that defines the view. The view contains the row resulting from the execution of this SELECT command.

WITH CHECK OPTION
> When this option is specified, all the insert and update operations are checked against the view's definition and are rejected when they do not satisfy the definition.

When you create a view, consider the following items:

- A view can only be created in the database in use.
- It is not possible to associate triggers, rules, and defaults to a view.
- A view can use data from another view.
- A view can be referenced by a stored procedure.
- It is not possible to create an index for a view.
- When more than one column of the view has the same name, they must be referenced by an alias or preceded by the name of the table to which they belong.
- The columns of a view are identical to the columns of the original table.

As an example, we will create a view that is identical to the view shown in the figure on the following page. The code shows the creation of a view called Test1. It has the title_id and Title columns from the Titles table, and pub_name from the Publishers table. The rows of both tables are synchronized through the WHERE clause, which returns the name of the publisher that has the same code in the pub_id field in both tables.

```
CREATE VIEW test1
AS
SELECT titles.title_id, titles.title, publishers.pub_name
FROM titles, publishers
WHERE titles.pub_id=publishers.pub_id;
```

Here is the result:

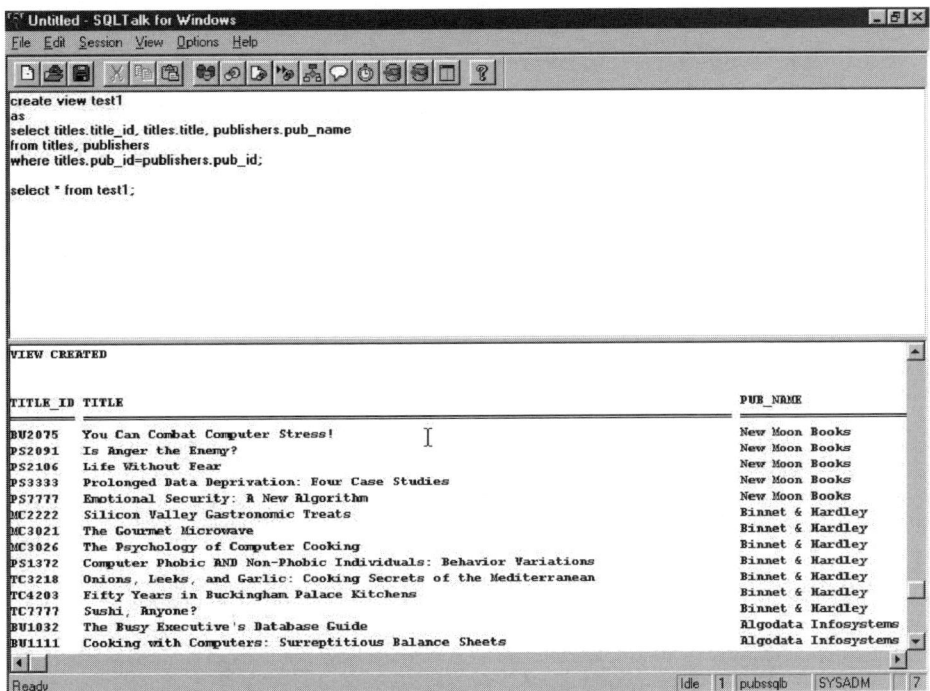

After a view is created, it can be queried, edited, or deleted just like a normal table.

Column Names

The view's columns have the same name as the original columns from the tables that form it. To create an alias, put the new name inside parentheses after the name of the original column. Some databases accept the AS option as in the command "SELECT column AS alias".

An alias is only necessary when the column is calculated, that is, based on expressions or constants, or when there are columns with the same name in the tables that form the view. Take a look at the next example:

Input:

```
CREATE VIEW test2
AS
SELECT titles.pub_id, titles.title, publishers.pub_id,
publishers.pub_name
```

```
FROM titles, publishers
WHERE titles.pub_id=publishers.pub_id;
```

Result:

Error: Column PUB_ID specified twice

The pub_id column, although specified with the name of the table before the name of the column, causes an error when the view is created. Although the pub_id field is redundant here since the columns have the same contents, in other situations columns from different tables may use the same name for columns containing different data. To create an alias for the column, specify a list of the names of columns that will receive (in the same order they are specified) the columns of the tables, as shown in the next example:

Input:

```
CREATE VIEW test2 (pub_code, title, pub_id, name)
AS
SELECT titles.pub_id, titles.title, publishers.pub_id,
publishers.pub_name
FROM titles, publishers
WHERE titles.pub_id=publishers.pub_id;
SELECT * FROM test2;
```

Result (partial):

PUB_CODE	TITLE	PUB_ID	NAME
0736	You Can Combat Computer Stress!	0736	New Moon Books
0736	Is Anger the Enemy?	0736	New Moon Books
0736	Life Without Fear	0736	New Moon Books
0736	Prolonged Data Deprivation: Four Case Studies	0736	New Moon Books
0736	Emotional Security: A New Algorithm	0736	New Moon Books
0877	Silicon Valley Gastronomic Treats	0877	Binnet & Hardl
0877	The Gourmet Microwave	0877	Binnet & Hardl
0877	The Psychology of Computer Cooking	0877	Binnet & Hardl
0877	Computer Phobic AND Non-Phobic Individuals: Behavior Variations	0877	Binnet & Hardl
0877	Onions, Leeks, and Garlic: Cooking Secrets of the Mediterranean	0877	Binnet & Hardl
0877	Fifty Years in Buckingham Palace Kitchens	0877	Binnet & Hardl
0877	Sushi, Anyone?	0877	Binnet & Hardl
1389	The Busy Executive's Database Guide	1389	Algodata Infos
1389	Cooking with Computers: Surreptitious Balance Sheets	1389	Algodata Infos
1389	Straight Talk About Computers	1389	Algodata Infos
1389	But Is It User Friendly?	1389	Algodata Infos

Querying a View

From the user's perspective, a view is a table like any other. You can use the SELECT command as you would in a table. In the next example, only the titles starting with the letter "T" are displayed in alphabetical and ascending order.

Input:

```
SELECT * FROM test1
WHERE title LIKE 'T%'
ORDER BY title;
```

Result:

```
TITLE_ID  TITLE                                 PUB_NAME
========  ====================================  ====================
BU1032    The Busy Executive's Database Guide   Algodata Infosystems
MC3021    The Gourmet Microwave                 Binnet & Hardley
MC3026    The Psychology of Computer Cooking    Binnet & Hardley
```

Deleting a View

When the view is deleted, its definition is deleted from the data dictionary. The original tables are not affected.

The command used to delete a view is DROP VIEW. The command must contain the view's name.

Syntax:

```
DROP VIEW <view_name>
```

Input:

```
DROP VIEW test2;
```

Result:

VIEW DROPPED.

Changing Data with a View

You can change the contents of the original table used to create a view by using the UPDATE and DELETE commands. However, this is only possible when the view uses columns from just one table. The next example creates a view with fields taken only from the Titles table. Then it updates the price of the book with code 1389. After that, it returns the original price of the book.

Input:

```
CREATE VIEW test2 as
SELECT title_id, price, title
FROM titles
WHERE pub_id='1389';

SELECT * FROM test2;

UPDATE test2
SET price=20
WHERE title_id='PC8888';
SELECT * FROM test2;

UPDATE test2
SET price=30
WHERE title_id='PC8888';
```

Result:

TITLE_ID	PRICE	TITLE
========	=====	==
BU1032	19.99	The Busy Executive's Database Guide
BU1111	11.95	Cooking with Computers: Surreptitious Balance Sheets
BU7832	19.99	Straight Talk About Computers
PC1035	22.95	But Is It User Friendly?
PC8888	20	Secrets of Silicon Valley
PC9999		Net Etiquette

6 ROWS SELECTED

1 ROW UPDATED

TITLE_ID	PRICE	TITLE
========	=====	==
BU1032	19.99	The Busy Executive's Database Guide
BU1111	11.95	Cooking with Computers: Surreptitious Balance Sheets
BU7832	19.99	Straight Talk About Computers

```
PC1035    22.95    But Is It User Friendly?
PC8888    30       Secrets of Silicon Valley
PC9999             Net Etiquette
```

6 ROWS SELECTED

1 ROW UPDATED

Using the CHECK OPTION Parameter

During the creation of a view you can use the CHECK OPTION parameter to restrict the type of updating that is possible in the view, based on the SELECT command that created it. For example, when a view is created based on the Titles table for books that cost at least $20, changes cannot be made that reduce the book's price to less than that value.

Input:

```
CREATE VIEW test3
AS
SELECT title_id, price, title
FROM titles WHERE price>=20
WITH CHECK OPTION;

SELECT * FROM test3;
```

Result:

```
TITLE_ID  PRICE   TITLE
========  =====   ======================================================
PC1035    22.95   But Is It User Friendly?
PC8888    20      Secrets of Silicon Valley
PS1372    21.59   Computer Phobic AND Non-Phobic Individuals: Behavior
                  Variations
TC3218    20.95   Onions, Leeks, and Garlic: Cooking Secrets of the
                  Mediterranean
```

Now let's try to change the price of the book with code PC8888 to 15.

Input:

```
UPDATE test3
SET price=15
WHERE title_id='PC8888'
```

Result:

`Error: Invalid data for this view`

Different databases may issue similar messages indicating that the value is invalid for that view.

Summary

In this chapter, you have seen that views are useful tools for offering a different perspective of information to different users. You learned how to create and delete a view, as well as how to create views with updating restrictions. In the next chapter, we will discuss a more advanced subject: embedded SQL.

Review Questions

1. What is a view?
2. What is the command (and its syntax) used to create a view?
3. What is the command (and its syntax) used to delete a view?
4. When it is possible to change the data of the original table referenced by a view?
5. What is the purpose of the CHECK OPTION clause?

Chapter 14
Embedded SQL

- Using embedded SQL
- Using a Centura application

Now that you have learned a lot about SQL, it's time for you to find out that the SQL language does not live alone. It is not possible to write an executable program solely in SQL. You have to create a program using a third- or fourth-generation language that allows you to embed the SQL code, or pass parameters so this code can be executed in the database.

How Embedded SQL Works

In order to use embedded SQL in another language, that language must provide support for the embedded SQL. In addition, you will have to master the host language that will store the embedded SQL code.

Inside the host language, rows containing special commands are inserted, generally with EXEC SQL, or through a function call. The commands specified in these lines are precompiled and passed to the host language. The host language then calls the SQL routines, passing and receiving parameters through the variables. The database, in turn, calls the low-level routines that activate the SQL engine inside the database, which receives the parameters and commands passed, executes them, and returns the desired information.

This chapter will not teach you how to create these applications in another language; that would require an entire book. However, we will show a practical application of the use of SQL embedded in another language.

Note On the companion CD, there is an application written in Centura, an evolution of SQLWindows, that accesses the tables of the Pubssqlb database. If you have this program installed, run it now, following the instructions provided in Appendix D.

The Application

This application, developed by Ana Paula Bonani of Centura Brasil, shows the initial screen for connecting with the database. In this screen the user must press the Connect button in order to connect to the Pubssqlb database, previously defined in the Database field using the user and password also previously defined in the User and Password fields. These three fields are write-protected, i.e., the user cannot change them. To exit the application, press the Cancel button.

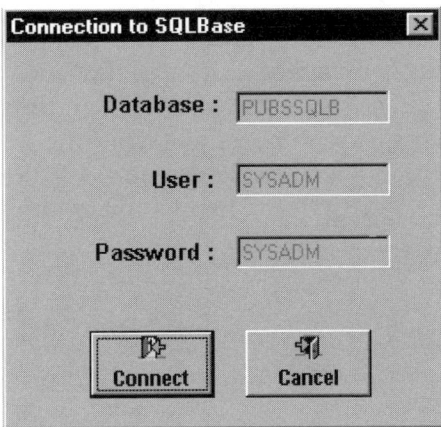

The next screen that appears is the main screen of the program.

This screen contains author data that is automatically loaded when the user presses the Connect button in the connection screen. From then on the user can navigate through the records using the First, Previous, Next, and Last buttons. When the user is positioned in the record of the first author registered and presses the Previous button, he or she receives a message saying that this is the first registered author and that there is no previous record. The same will happen when the user is positioned in the record of the last registered author and presses the Next button. To view details from books published by a specific author, navigate to the record for the desired author and press the Books button. The first registered book for this author will be shown. When the author has no books published, a message appears saying that there are no books for the author. To finish the application, press the Exit button. Next is the Books screen:

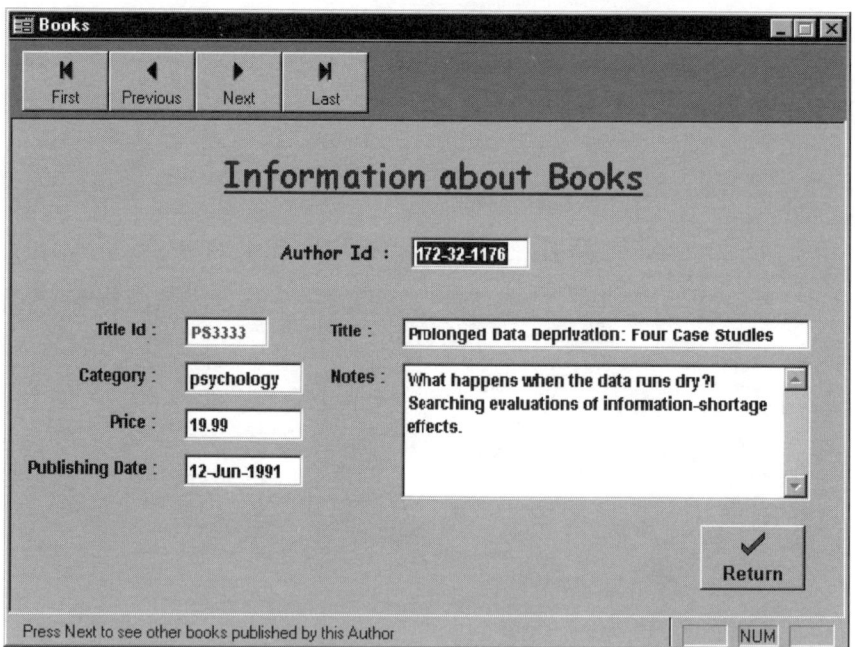

This screen shows the code for the author who was previously selected in the Authors screen, and details of the first book found for that author. To view other books by the same author, use the First, Previous, Next, and Last buttons. When the user is positioned in the first registered book and presses the Previous button, a message appears stating that this is the first registered book for this author, and that there are no previous records. The same thing will happen when the user is positioned in the last book registered and presses the Next button. Otherwise, several books of the same author will be displayed. To return to the Authors screen, press the Return button.

Behind the Scenes

This application was created in two steps. The first step used Centura's form designer to create all the screens used in the application. The next screen shows the creation of the Authors screen.

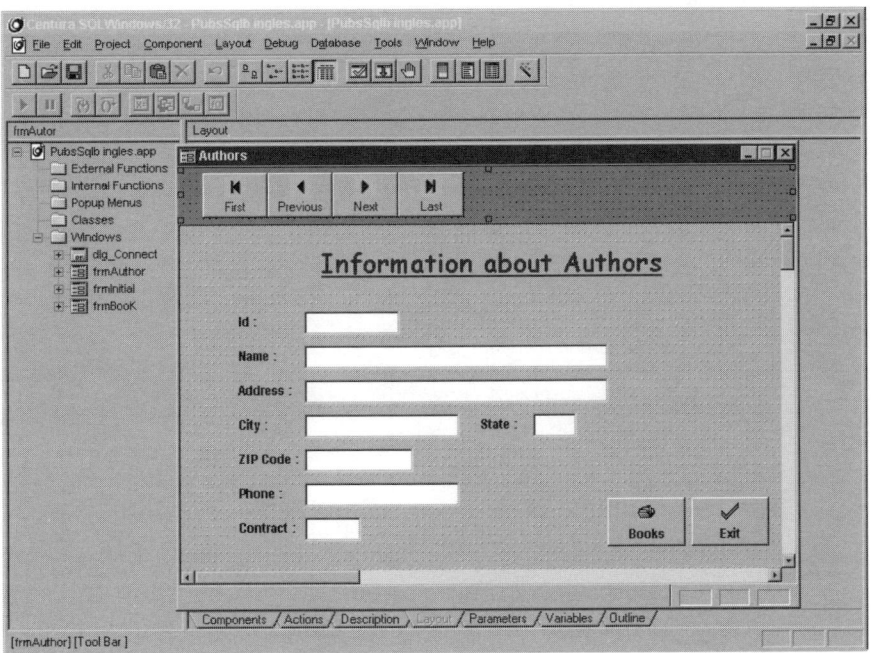

Once the interface was defined, the code associated with the events and objects was created. An example is the PopulaFormWindow function as shown on the following page.

The objective of this function is to load data from authors who are registered in the Pubssqlb database as soon as the user presses the Connect button in the SQLBase connection screen. This function prepares, compiles, and executes the SELECT command that selects the contents of the fields in the Authors table, and shows them in the corresponding fields in the Authors table, using the INTO clause.

Chapter 14

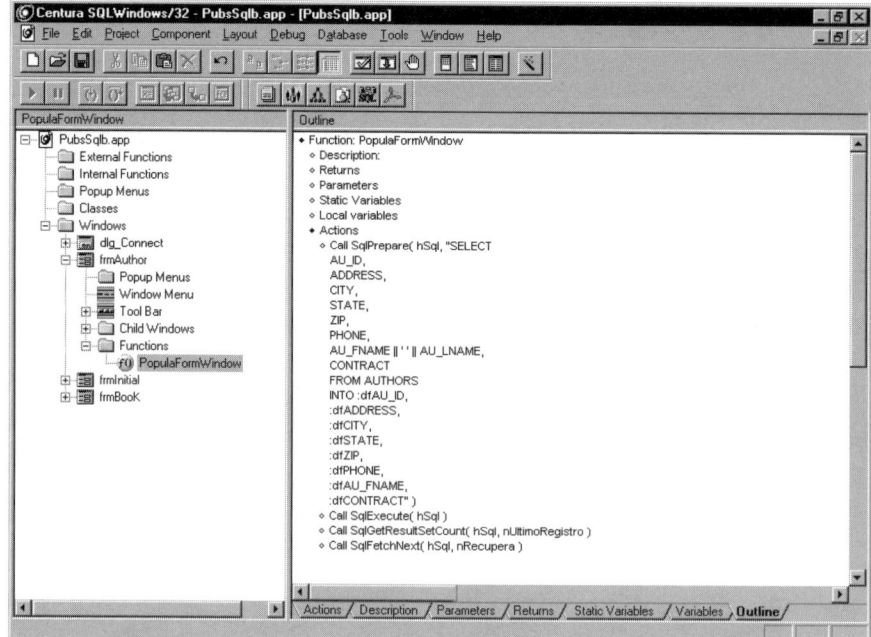

Another example is the PopulaChildTable function, shown on the following page.

This function selects the records in the Titleauthors table related to the records of the Authors and Titles tables of the Pubssqlb database, and shows its contents in the corresponding fields of the Titles table, using the SELECT command. This command selects just the books published by the selected author. When the selection is complete, a test is run to check if there are books published by that author. If so, the books published by the author are recovered. Otherwise, a message is sent saying that this author has no books published.

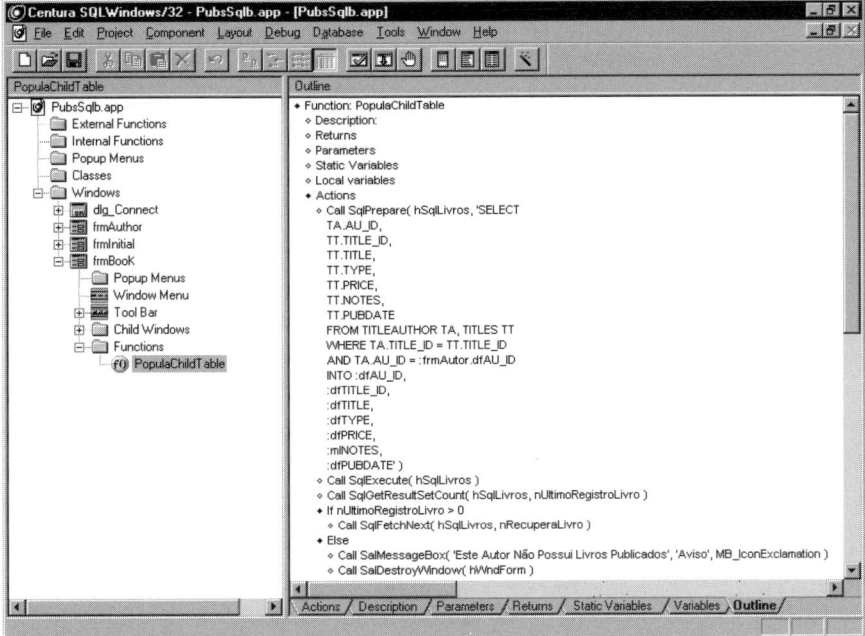

Summary

An application that accesses a relational database invariably will use the SQL language at some point of the process of recovery or creation of data. To the user, it is just a well-designed and pleasant query screen. To the developer, it means rows and more rows of code written in SQL and another language that combine to take advantage of all the potential of the relational databases.

The next chapter discusses miscellaneous SQL topics, including synonyms, privileges, and transactions.

Chapter 15
Miscellaneous

- Synonyms
- Users, privileges, and roles
- Transactions

In this chapter we will cover three miscellaneous topics that vary widely among the dialects, but which are important for learning other SQL commands or database extensions. The topics covered are:

- Synonyms
- Roles and privileges
- Transactions

Synonyms

Synonyms are a simpler way to access tables and other database objects by using an alternate or shortcut name. A *synonym* is an alias for an object. When a synonym is created, a reference to the original object is made. For example, when a synonym is created for a table, Oracle will associate the address of the table to the synonym instead of creating a duplicate of the table.

Synonyms have many advantages, the most important of which may be that they hide the identity of the object that is being referenced. When the object is changed or moved, all that is needed is to update the synonym, rather than having to change several direct references. Often, the security aspect is not the most important one. A table with an extensive name that belongs to a different scheme from that of the user can be abbreviated with a synonym, making the execution of the commands much easier.

Synonyms can be created for several objects, including views, snapshots, sequences, procedure function packages, or even other synonyms.

Synonyms can be public and visible to all users, or private and available only to the user who created it. In Oracle a synonym can be used to replace an object in the following SQL commands (check your dialect's restrictions):

SELECT
INSERT
DELETE
GRANT
COMMENT
UPDATE
EXPLAIN PLAN
LOCK TABLE

REVOKE

AUDIT

NOAUDIT

If the user tries to create a synonym with an existing name under another synonym or other database object, a warning message is issued and the synonym will not be created.

Syntax for SQLBase:

```
CREATE [PUBLIC] SYNONYM synonym_name
FOR [TABLE] object_name
    [EXTERNAL FUNCTION]
    [PROCEDURE]
    [COMMAND]
```

Arguments:

PUBLIC Allows you to access a table, external function, stored command, or stored procedure through a synonym, without the need to qualify the object name with the owner's identifier. You must be the object's owner or be a DBA or SYSADM in order to create a synonym.

synonym_name
    The name of the synonym to be created.

TABLE When the type of object is omitted, the default is TABLE.

object_name The name of the object type can be a table, view, external function, stored command, or stored procedure. These objects must exist in the database.

EXTERNAL FUNCTION
    You must specify this clause after the FOR keyword when you create a synonym for an external function.

PROCEDURE You must specify this clause after the FOR keyword when you create a synonym for a stored procedure.

COMMAND You must specify this clause after the FOR keyword when you create a synonym for a stored procedure.

Examples:

```
CREATE SYNONYM employee FOR empxx1;

SELECT * FROM employee;
SELECT * FROM empxx1;
```

Users, Privileges, and Roles

An important concept for the database administrator to understand concerns the creation of users. Anyone who wants to access a database must be registered as a database user and have privileges established for him or her as to the tasks that he or she will be allowed to perform in the database. Roles and privileges are important for security purposes to restrict access to databases.

Users

Controlling access to the database is one of the main tasks of an administrator. To perform this database control, administrators use a mechanism that allows registering a person that is then called user. Each registered user receives an access password that must be provided in certain situations. Individual privileges are then granted to each user. In Oracle, a role, which consists of a group of privileges that can be granted simultaneously to a user, can be granted. These concepts are discussed in this section.

Creating a User

The CREATE USER command is responsible for the creation of new users. It allows the allocation of maximum and minimum sizes of space for the user, as well as choosing which tablespaces must be used.

Syntax:

```
CREATE USER user IDENTIFIED BY password/ EXTERNALLY.
DEFAULT TABLESPACE tablespace
TEMPORARY TABLESPACE tablespace
QUOTA  K/M/ UNLIMITED  ON TABLESPACE name
PROFILE profile
```

Arguments:

IDENTIFIED BY
    Must be followed by the user password or the word EXTERNALLY, which tells Oracle to look for the password used in the operating system.

DEFAULT TABLESPACE
    Identifies the tablespace used for the user's objects. When omitted, Oracle assumes the tablespace System.

TEMPORARY TABLESPACE
: Identifies the tablespace used for the temporary objects of the database.

QUOTA
: Specifies the maximum amount of space in the tablespace in KB or MB.

PROFILE
: Attributes the values stored in the profile specified for the user. When omitted, assumes the profile called Default. A profile is a file containing limits of database use for a user. Similar to a role, multiple users can use a profile.

To create a user you must have the proper privileges. The next example shows the user System creating a user with the simplest form of the command.

```
SQL> connect
Enter user-name: system
Enter password: *******
Connected.
SQL> CREATE USER arnold IDENTIFIED BY schwartz;

User created.
```

You can use one of the tables in the data dictionary in order to check the database's users. The name of this table is ALL_USERS.

```
SQL> SELECT * FROM all_users;

USERNAME      USER_ID    CREATED
========      =======    =========
SYS           0          23-APR-96
SYSTEM        5          23-APR-96
SCOTT         8          23-APR-96
DEMO          9          23-APR-96
PO7           10         29-APR-96
CINDY         12         18-MAY-97
ARNOLD        13         18-MAY-97

7 rows selected.
```

Deleting a User

A database user is removed with the DROP USER command. It removes both the user and all the objects contained in the user's schema. In this case it is necessary to specify the CASCADE clause of the command.

Oracle also removes all the referential integrity associated with the objects of the removed user.

Syntax:

```
DROP USER name <CASCADE>
```

The next example shows the removal of user Arnold.

```
SQL> DROP USER arnold;

User dropped.

SQL> SELECT * FROM all_users;

USERNAME  USER_ID  CREATED
========  =======  =========
SYS       0        23-APR-96
SYSTEM    5        23-APR-96
SCOTT     8        23-APR-96
DEMO      9        23-APR-96
PO7       10       29-APR-96
CINDY     12       18-MAY-97

6 ROWS SELECTED
```

Privileges

A *privilege* is an authorization given to a user to access and manipulate database objects. For example, a user may be permitted to select tables, although he or she cannot change the tables. Another user may be able to both read and update, or even change the structure of tables and other objects. Since all the manipulation of a database is done through SQL commands, a privilege grants a user the right to use certain SQL commands.

There are two types of privileges: system privileges and object privileges. A *system privilege* is the right or permission to execute a database action in some specific type of database object. There are more than 70 types of privileges associated to the actions of the database. The name of the privilege is similar to the name of the action it executes. For example, the ALTER TABLE privilege allows the user to change a table. Examples of system privileges are listed in Table 15-1.

Table 15-1. System Privileges

Action	Privilege	Action	Privilege
Analyze	Analyze any	Session	Create session
			Alter session
			Restrict session
Audit	Audit any		
	Audit system		
Cluster	Create cluster	Snapshot	Create snapshot
	Create any cluster		Create any snapshot
	Alter any cluster		Alter any snapshot
	Drop any cluster		Drop any snapshot
Database	Alter database		
Database Link	Create database link		
Index	Create any index	Synonym	Create synonym
	Alter any index		Create any synonym
	Drop any index		Drop any synonym
Privilege	Grant any privilege	System	Alter system
Procedure	Create procedure	Table	Create table
	Create any procedure		Create any table
	Alter any procedure		Alter any table
	Drop any procedure		Back up any table
	Execute any procedure		Drop any table
			Lock any table
			Comment any table
			Select any table
			Insert any table
			Update any table
			Delete any table

Table 15-1. System Privileges (continued)

Action	Privilege	Action	Privilege
Profile	Create profile	Tablespace	Create tablespace
	Alter profile		Alter tablespace
	Drop profile		Manage tablespace
	Alter resource cost		Drop tablespace
			Unlimited tablespace
Public database link	Create public database link	Transaction	Force transaction
	Drop public database link		Force any transaction
Public synonym	Create public synonym		
	Drop public synonym		
Role	Create role	Trigger	Create trigger
	Alter any role		Create any trigger
	Drop any role		Alter any trigger
	Grant any role		Drop any trigger
Rollback segment	Create rollback segment	User	Create user
	Alter rollback segment		Become user
	Drop rollback segment		Alter user
			Drop user
Sequence	Create sequence	View	Create view
	Create any sequence		Create any view
	Alter any sequence		Drop any view
	Drop any sequence		
	Select any sequence		

An *object privilege* is the right to execute certain actions in a specific object, such as the right to include a row in a specific table. The privileges of the object do not apply to all the database's objects. Triggers, procedures, indexes, database links, and clusters do not have object privileges. Examples of object privileges are listed in Table 15-2.

Table 15-2. Object Privileges

Privilege	Object
Alter	Tables, sequences
Delete	Tables, views
Execute	Procedures
Index	Tables
Insert	Tables, views
Reference	Tables
Select	Tables, views, sequences
Update	Tables, views

When a user creates an object, only that user can view it. For another user to have access to it, the user owner must grant privileges to the user or role that will access the object.

Granting Privileges and Roles

To grant a privilege or role to a role, use the following syntax:

```
GRANT role privilege_name TO user/role/ PUBLIC
      WITH ADMIN OPTION
```

This example grants the CONNECT and RESOURCE roles to the Basic1 role:

```
SQL> GRANT connect, resource TO basic1;

Grant succeeded.
```

A variation of the GRANT command allows you to assign object privileges to a user or role. The privileges granted can be the following: ALTER, DELETE, EXECUTE, INSERT, INDEX, REFERENCE, SELECT, and UPDATE. The objects that can grant privileges are tables, views, sequences, snapshots, and synonyms.

Syntax:

```
GRANT  privilege_name/ALL PRIVILEGES  <columns> ON schema.object TO user/role/ PUBLIC
       WITH GRANT OPTION
```

Arguments:

ALL PRIVILEGES
: Assigns all the privileges of the object.

<columns>
: Specifies the columns to which the privilege (only INSERT, UPDATE, and REFERENCE) is being granted.

PUBLIC
: Grants the privilege to all database users.

GRANT OPTION
: Allows the user/role that receives the privilege to grant it to other users.

The next example shows user Scott granting the SELECT privilege so user Arnold can access the Dept table.

```
SQL> connect
Enter user-name: scott
Enter password: *****
Connected.
SQL> GRANT SELECT on scott.dept TO arnold;

Grant succeeded.

SQL> connect
Enter user-name: arnold
Enter password: ********
Connected.

SQL> SELECT * FROM scott.dept;

DEPTNO    DNAME         LOC
======    ==========    ========
10        ACCOUNTING    NEW YORK
20        RESEARCH      DALLAS
30        SALES         CHICAGO
40        OPERATIONS    BOSTON

SQL>
```

Revoking Privileges

To revoke a privilege, use the REVOKE command. In order to revoke a system privilege, it must have been given the ADMIN option. Let's try to revoke the privilege granted to user Arnold which did not receive this option.

```
SQL> REVOKE basic1 FROM arnold;
REVOKE basic1 FROM arnold
       *
ERROR at line 1:
ORA-01932: ADMIN option not granted for role 'BASIC1'
```

An error occurred because the role did not receive ADMIN when it was granted. We connect as SYSTEM user and assign again the CONNECT and RESOURCE roles as the Basic1 role, now with the ADMIN option.

```
SQL> connect
Enter user-name: system
Enter password: *******
Connected.
SQL> GRANT connect, resource TO basic1 WITH ADMIN OPTION ;

Grant succeeded.
```

Next we use the REVOKE command to revoke the basic1 role of user Arnold.

```
SQL> REVOKE basic1 FROM arnold;

Revoke succeeded.
```

To check the functionality of a command, we tried to connect as Arnold. Oracle verified that Arnold does not have the CONNECT role anymore, and did not allow the connection to the database.

```
SQL> connect
Enter user-name: arnold
Enter password: ********
ERROR: ORA-01045: user ARNOLD lacks CREATE SESSION privilege; logon denied
```

Object privileges granted to a user can also be revoked. Let's say user Scott received from user Cindy the SELECT privilege for the Dept table. Now we will revoke this privilege using a SQL command. To revoke a privilege, you must connect as the user who granted that privilege. A user cannot grant or revoke privileges to himself. In this case we have to connect as user Scott.

```
SQL> connect
Enter user-name: scott
Enter password: *****
Connected.
```

Next the REVOKE command must be used specifying the privilege, object, and user that will be revoked.

```
SQL> REVOKE SELECT ON scott.dept FROM cindy;
```

Revoke succeeded.

To see if the revoke worked, we connect as the user Cindy and try to access the Scott.dept table. Because this privilege does not exist, Cindy cannot access the table.

```
SQL> connect
Enter user-name: cindy
Enter password: *******
Connected.
SQL> SELECT * FROM scott.dept;
SELECT * FROM scott.dept
              *
ERROR at line 1:
ORA-00942: table or view does not exist
```

Note that only one SYSADM user can revoke the authority DBA of another user. When the RESOURCE or DBA authority is removed from a user, this does not take effect until the next time the user connects.

Syntax:

```
REVOKE authority level FROM auth_id
```

Arguments:

<authority level>
> The following authority levels can be revoked by the SYSADM:

SYSADM	This level of authority cannot be removed.
DBA	Revoking this level of authority means that the user cannot create or delete tables, or grant or revoke privileges to users. However, he or she maintains the CONNECT privilege.
RESOURCE	Revoking this level of authority means that the user does not have the right to create or delete tables anymore. However, he or she maintains the CONNECT privilege.

CONNECT	Revoking this level of authority means that the user cannot access the database anymore. All the privileges related to tables and views must be removed from the user before the CONNECT authority can be revoked.

Roles

A *role* is a group of privileges. Thus, instead of granting eight privileges to a user, you can create a role that receives those eight privileges and then assign the role to a user. The use of roles simplifies administration.

Oracle 7 has many predefined roles, such as CONNECT, RESOURCE, DBA, EXP_FULL_DATABASE, and IMP_FULL_DATABASE. In addition, the user can create other roles that satisfy the needs of his or her applications.

Below are Oracle's predefined users, passwords, and roles:

User	Password	Role
SCOTT	TIGER	CONNECT and RESOURCE
SYSTEM	MANAGER	DBA
SYS	SYS*	CONNECT, RESOURCE, DBA, EXP_FULL_DATABASE, IMP_FULL_DATABASE
DEMO	DEMO	CONNECT and RESOURCE
PO7	PO7	DBA

* If you are using Windows 97, the password for SYS user is the Windows serial number without the hyphens. This number may be obtained by clicking the System icon in the Control Panel folder. It appears after the user identification, with a format similar to "28877-411-1357921-04810". The SYS user is the most powerful of all the users. Therefore, use it only when necessary, since it can execute actions that may compromise the database or its contents.

Here is an explanation of what each role does:

Role	Privilege
CONNECT	Allow access to the database
RESOURCE	Allows access to the database and the creation of tables, sequences, procedures, triggers, indexes, and clusters.

Role	Privilege
DBA	All the system's prileges. It allows granting the privilege to other users.
EXP_FULL_DATABASE	Export the database.
IMP_FULL_DATABASE	Import the database.

To create a role, a user must have the CREATE ROLE privilege. When a role is created by the user, he or she receives the ADMIN OPTION which allows the user to grant the role to other roles or users, remove the role granted to the user/role, change the access to the role, and delete the role.

Creating Roles

The SQL command used to create a role is CREATE ROLE.

Syntax:

```
CREATE ROLE name <IDENTIFIED BY password / EXTERNALLY >
```

Arguments:

IDENTIFIED BY
> Asks for a verification password for the user. You can provide the Oracle password or use the EXTERNALLY option to obtain the password from the operating system.

```
SQL> CREATE ROLE basic1;
Role created.
```

Granting Roles

To grant a role, simply use the GRANT command followed by the role and name of the user:

```
SQL> GRANT basic1 TO arnold;

Grant succeeded.

SQL> connect
Enter user-name: arnold
Enter password: ********
Connected.
SQL>
```

Viewing Roles

Oracle has some special tables to control privileges and roles. One of these tables is called USER_ROLE_PRIVS. It shows the roles assigned to the current user.

```
SQL> SELECT * FROM user_role_privs;

USERNAME   GRANTED_ROLE   ADM  DEF  OS_
========   ============   ====  ===  ==
ARNOLD     BASIC1         NO   YES  NO

SQL>
```

Deleting Roles

The command responsible for deleting a role is DROP ROLE. To remove a role a user must have the system privilege DROP ANY ROLE or the role must be created with the option ADMIN OPTION.

Syntax:

```
DROP ROLE role
```

The next example sequence removes the Basic1 role. When removing a role, Oracle updates all the grants of the role and updates roles and users that depend on the role being removed. After removing the Basic1 role that was granted to user Arnold, we tried to connect with this user. However, Oracle prevented the access since the user does not have the access privilege anymore.

```
SQL> connect
Enter user-name: system
Enter password: *******
Connected.
SQL> DROP ROLE basic1;

Role dropped.

SQL> connect
Enter user-name: arnold
Enter password: ********
ERROR: ORA-01045: user ARNOLD lacks CREATE SESSION privilege; logon denied
```

This section has demonstrated the importance of mastering the concepts of roles and privileges. They are one of the main methods of controlling database access and limiting the operations that can be executed by a user or a group of users. As a developer, you do not need to worry about this subject. But if you are a database administrator, the importance of roles and privileges is crucial for security.

Transactions

Transactions are important for maintaining the data integrity of a database. A *transaction* is a sequence of operations performed by the database as a unique work unit. A work unit or logical work unit needs the four ACID properties (atomicity, consistency, isolation, and durability) to be considered a transaction.

Atomicity

Atomicity is the fact that all changes in data are performed; if any one change fails, none are performed.

Consistency

When a transaction is completed, it must leave all data in a consistent state. In other words, the database must be continually consistent.

Isolation

The changes made by simultaneous transactions must be isolated from the changes made by other transactions. That is, a transaction sees a piece of data in the state it was in before the transaction and the piece of data after the transaction is concluded, but never in an intermediate state. If the transaction received the value 5 and returns it as 10, these are the values that it will see even if another transaction has changed the value to 7.

Durability

This means that the effects of the transaction are permanent after its completion.

Imagine an operation involving thousands of records in a table. In the middle of the operation a software problem occurs, the power goes out, or the processing is interrupted for another reason. Let's say the prices in a product table were being changed. When the process is interrupted, part of the table has been updated, while the other part has not. How do you know which records are updated? What do you do to return the database to its previous status? The more complex the system, the more difficult this task is. Related tables that require the deletion of rows from other tables can end up orphans since the rows of the master table may have been deleted while the ones in the child table may not.

Using the concept of transaction the database makes a record in a log file of all the operations that are being performed from the moment the transaction starts. When the process starts, it registers a control mark saying that the transaction is not complete. When the transaction ends, it changes the mark to "transaction complete." During restoration of the database, the mark indicates that the transaction was not complete and the database, through a specific command, can return the data to the beginning of the transaction.

The SQL programmer is responsible for initiating and terminating the transaction in the points of the program that force the logical data consistency. He or she must establish the sequence of commands and changes according to the business rules of the company for that operation.

Basically, there are three commands used to control the transaction. COMMIT and ROLLBACK are available in most dialects and have relatively standardized syntax. BEGIN TRANSACTION, on the other hand, varies.

BEGIN TRANSACTION (SQL Server 7)

BEGIN TRANSACTION indicates the initial points of an explicit local transaction. BEGIN TRANSACTION increments @@TRANCOUNT of a unit.

Syntax:

```
BEGIN TRAN[SACTION] [transaction_name | @tran_name_variable]
```

Arguments:

transaction_name
: The name assigned to the transaction. It must satisfy the rules established for the identifiers. Use transaction names only in the most external pair of the nested instructions BEGIN...COMMIT or BEGIN...ROLLBACK.

@tran_name_variable
: This is the name of a variable defined by the user containing a valid transaction name. The variable must be declared with a data type of char, varchar, nchar, or nvarchar.

ROLLBACK

This command terminates a current transaction. When a ROLLBACK command is executed, SQLBase aborts the current transaction. This restores the database up to the state it was in before the last COMMIT or ROLLBACK or, if this has not occurred, up to the moment of connection by the user.

Syntax:

```
ROLLBACK [savepoint_identifier] [TRANSACTION <id> FORCE]
```

Arguments:

savepoint_identifier
: When this marker is specified, the transaction rolls back until this point. The marker is put inside a transaction with the SAVEPOINT command. When this marker does not exist, the entire transaction is rolled back and an error message is sent.

TRANSACTION <ID> FORCE
: This clause forces a manual ROLLBACK in a questionable distributed transaction. You should only force a rollback as a last resource. The value <ID> is the global identifier of the transaction in the Sysparttrans table.

COMMIT

This command makes all the changes performed in the database since the last COMMIT or ROLLBACK, or since the initial connection made by the user if no commands have been performed.

The COMMIT operation applies to all the SQL commands, including the definition commands (CREATE, DROP, ALTER) and control commands (GRANT, UPDATE, DELETE).

The "locks" are always freed after a COMMIT, unless the cursor preservation mode is active.

Syntax:

```
COMMIT [WORK] [TRANSACTION <id> FORCE]
```

Arguments:

WORK   This is provided for compatibility with DB2, but has no effect.

TRANSACTION <ID> FORCE
            This clause forces a manual COMMIT of a doubtful distributed transaction.

In this SQL Server 7 example, all the royalties for the computer books are increased by 20%.

```
DECLARE @TranName VARCHAR(20)
SELECT @TranName = 'MyTransaction'
BEGIN TRANSACTION @TranName
GO
USE pubs
GO
UPDATE roysched
SET royalty = royalty * 1.20
WHERE title_id LIKE 'Pc%'
GO
COMMIT TRANSACTION MyTransaction
GO
```

This example shows the advance to be paid to an author when the annual sales of a book exceed $6,000.

```
BEGIN TRANSACTION
USE pubs
GO
UPDATE titles
SET advance = advance * 1.25
WHERE ytd_sales > 6000
GO
COMMIT
```

Summary

The topics discussed in this chapter—synonyms, roles and privileges, and transactions—are out of the scope of standard SQL, but are important for a SQL programmer to know. This chapter concludes the section on the basics of SQL.

Now we turn to the appendixes, which contain summaries of SQL functions, commands, and data types, and instructions for using the companion CD-ROM.

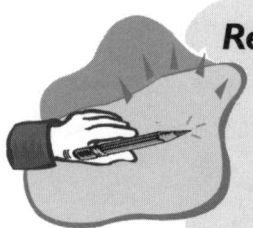

Review Questions

1. What are synonyms?
2. What are public synonyms?
3. Write the basic syntax of the command used to create synonyms.
4. What is the command (and its syntax) used to create a user?
5. What is the command (and its syntax) used to to delete a user?
6. What are privileges?
7. What is the command (and its syntax) used to create privileges?
8. What are roles?
9. What are the commands used to create and delete a role?

Appendix A
Functions

This appendix contains a summary of the functions supported by SQL Server 7, Oracle 8, and SQLBase 7 databases. Many functions have the same name and work identically in more than one of the SQL dialects.

Name	SQL Server 7	Oracle	SQLBase	Returns/Executes
ABS	X	X	@ABS	Absolute value
ACOS	X	X	@ACOS	Arc cosine
ADD_MONTHS(d,n)		X		Given the date d, returns the date in n months
ALL	X			True when the comparison of a scalar value to a set of columns is true
APP_NAME	X			The name of the program for the current session
ASCII	X	X		The ASCII code of the expression's leftmost character
ASIN	X	X	@ASIN	Arc sine
ATAN	X	X	@ATAN	Arc tangent of the second quadrant

Name	SQL Server 7	Oracle	SQLBase	Returns/Executes
ATAN2	ATN2	X	@ATAN2	Arc tangent of the fourth quadrant
AVG	X			The average of items
BFILENAME		X		A bfile locator associated to a binary file of blob type
CAST	X			Converts the expression to a specified data type
CEILING	X	CEIL		The smaller integer number greater than or equal to the argument
CHAR	X		@CHAR	An ASCII character
CHARINDEX	X			The initial position of the first argument inside the second argument
CHARTOROWID		X		Converts a value of char or varchar2 type to the data type rowid
@CHOOSE			@CHOOSE	Selects the value of a list based in a correlation
@CODE			@CODE	ASCII decimal code of the first character in a string
COL_LENGTH	X			The length defined for a column
COL_NAME	X			The name of the column in the specified table
COLUMNPROPERTY	X			Information referring to a procedure or column parameter
CONCAT(char1, char2)		X		Returns the argument char1 concatenated with char2
CONTAINSTABLE	X			An empty table or one containing lines of different types referring to specified search arguments

Functions

Name	SQL Server 7	Oracle	SQLBase	Returns/Executes
CONVERT		X		Converts a string from one set of characters to another
COS	X	X	@COS	Cosine
COSH		X		Hyperbolic cosine of the argument
COT	X			Cotangent
COUNT	X	X		Number of non-null arguments
@CTERM			@CTERM	Period necessary to obtain gains in the future
CURRENT_TIMESTAMP	X			The current date and hour of the system
CURRENT_USER	X			The current user
CURSOR_STATUS	X			Returns an integer that indicates the result of a procedure
DATABASEPROPERTY	X			The value of the specified database's property
DATALENGTH	X			The number of bytes used to represent the argument
@DATE			@DATE	Converts the value to data type
DATEADD	X			A new value of datetime type resulting from the addition of the specified value to the date
DATEDIFF	X			Returns the number of crossed boundaries between dates
DATENAME	X			A string representing the specified data range
DATEPART	X			An integer representing the specified data range
@DATETOCHAR			@DATETOCHAR	Edits the value of data type

Appendix A

Name	SQL Server 7	Oracle	SQLBase	Returns/Executes
@DATEVALUE			@DATEVALUE	Edits the value of data type
DAY	X		@DAY	Day of the month
DB_NAME	X			The name of the database
@DECIMAL			@DECIMAL	Decimal value of a hexadecimal string
@DECODE			@DECODE	Given an expression, it returns a string
DEGREES	X			The angle in degrees based on the argument specified in radians
DEREF		X		The reference to the specified object
DIFFERENCE	X			A value representing the SOUNDEX difference between the arguments
DUMP		X		Returns a value of type varchar2 with the data type code, size in bytes, and internal representation of the argument
EMPTY_[B|C]LOB		X		Returns a locator blob that can be used to initiate a variable
@EXACT			@EXACT	Compares two strings
EXP	X	X	@EXP	Returns the natural logarithm base (e) to the power x
@FACTORIAL			@FACTORIAL	Factorial
FILE_ID	X			The identification number of the file
FILE_NAME	X			The logical name of the file
FILEGROUP_ID	X			The identification number of the file group
FILEGROUP_NAME	X			The name of the file group

Name	SQL Server 7	Oracle	SQLBase	Returns/Executes
FILEGROUPPROPERTY	X			The value of the property referring to the group of files
FILEPROPERTY	X			The value of the file property
@FIND			@FIND	Position inside string1 that occurs in string2
FLOOR	X	X		Returns the smallest integer equal to or smaller than n
FORMATMESSAGE	X			Constructs a message based in a system message
FREETEXT	X			Looks for columns containing the type of data specified
FREETEXTTABLE	X			An empty table or one containing lines referring to the data types used as arguments
FULLTEXTCATALOGPROPERTY	X			Information on the catalog properties
FULLTEXTSERVICEPROPERTY	X			Service properties of current search
@FV			@FV	Future value obtained from a series of equal payments
GETANSINULL	X			Returns the default nullity for the database in use
GETDATE	X			The current date and hour of the system
GREATEST		X		Returns the greatest value in the list of expressions
@HEX			@HEX	Hexadecimal string of a decimal number
HEXTORAW		X		Raw type value of a hexadecimal string

Name	SQL Server 7	Oracle	SQLBase	Returns/Executes
HOST_ID	X			The identification number of the workstation
HOST_NAME	X			The name of the workstation
@HOUR			@HOUR	Hour of the day
IDENT_INCR	X			The incremental value specified during the creation of the column
IDENT_SEED	X			The seed value specified during the creation of an identity column
IDENTITY	X			Creates an identity column in a table
@IF			@IF	Tests number and returns 1 when true and 2 when false
INDEX_COL	X			The name of the indexed column
INDEXPROPERTY	X			The value of the index property of the specified table
INITCAP(char)		X		Returns the first letter of the argument in uppercase and the remaining in lowercase
INSTBR		X		The same as INSTR, except that n and the return value are expressed in bytes, rather than in characters
INSTR		X		Searches char1 beginning with its nth character for the nth occurrence of char2 and returns the position of the character in char1 that is the first character of this occurrence
@INT			@INT	Integer part
IS_MEMBER	X			Indicates that the user is a member of the group or role

Name	SQL Server 7	Oracle	SQLBase	Returns/Executes
IS_SRVROLEMEMBER	X			Indicates whether the user login is from a member of the specified role
ISDATE	X			Returns 1 when the variable is of date type; otherwise it returns zero
@ISNA			@ISNA	True when the argument is null
ISNULL	X			Replaces the null value with the specified value
ISNUMERIC	X			Returns 1 when the evaluated expression results in number; otherwise returns zero
LAST_DAY		X		The last day of the month
LEAST		X		Returns the smallest argument in the list of arguments
LEFT	X		@LEFT	Replaces the leftmost string
LEN	X			The number of characters instead of the number of bytes in a string
LENGTH		X	@LENGTH	Size of a string
LENGTHB		X		The same as length, but the arguments are specified in bytes
@LICS			@LICS	Order using a set of international characters
LN			@LN	Natural logarithm base (e) of x (positive)
LOG	X	X	@LOG	Logarithm of x in base 10
LOG10	X			The logarithm base 10 of the argument
LOWER	X	X	@LOWER	Turns uppercase into lowercase

Name	SQL Server 7	Oracle	SQLBase	Returns/Executes
LPAD(char1,n [,char2])		X		Returns char1 with the size n and with the initial positions filled with char2
LTRIM	X	X		Returns the expression with all the initial spaces deleted
MAKE_REF(table, key)		X		Creates a reference (ref) to a row with a view of the object, using key as the primary key
MAX	X	X	X	Maximum value for the arguments
@MEDIAN			@MEDIAN	Returns the average value in a list of values
@MICROSECOND			@MICROSECOND	Value in microseconds
@MID			@MID	Returns a string, beginning with the character in the initial position
MIN	X	X	X	Smallest value of the arguments
@MINUTE			@MINUTE	Minutes of the hour
MOD			@MOD	The remainder of the division x/y
MONTH	X		@MONTH	Month of the year
@MONTHBEG			@MONTHBEG	First day of the month
MONTHS_BETWEEN		X		The number of months between two specified dates
NCHAR	X			The Unicode character relating to the argument
NEW_TIME(d, z1, z2)		X		Date and hour of timezone z2 corresponding to the timezone z1
NEWID	X			Creates an exclusive value of uniqueidentifier type

Name	SQL Server 7	Oracle	SQLBase	Returns/Executes
NEXT_DAY		X		The first working day after the specified date
NLS_CHARSET_DECL_LEN		X		The number of characters of a column type nchar
NLS_CHARSET_ID		X		The identification number of the set of characters referring to the name provided
NLS_CHARSET_NAME		X		The name of the NLS character set of the specified code
NLS_INITCAP		X		Puts the first letter of each word in uppercase
NLS_LOWER		X		Lowercases the argument
NLSSORT		X		Returns the string of bytes used to order char
NLS_UPPER		X		Uppercases the argument
@NOW			@NOW	Current date and hour
NULLIF	X			The null value when two expressions are equivalent
@NULLVALUE			@NULLVALUE	Returns a string of numbers specified by y when x is null
NVL(expr1, expr2)		X		Expr2 when expr1 is null or expr1 when expr1 is true
OBJECT_ID	X			The identification number of the database's object
OBJECT_NAME	X			Returns the name of the database's object
OBJECTPROPERTY	X			Information on the properties of the specified object
OPENQUERY	X			Runs the query in the specified server

Name	SQL Server 7	Oracle	SQLBase	Returns/Executes
OPENROWSET	X			Runs a connection to remote data
PARSENAME	X			Returns the specified part of an object's name
PATINDEX	X			The initial position in the first occurrence of a default in an expression
PERMISSIONS	X			A value containing a bitmap that indicates the permissions for object instructions or columns for the final user
PI	X		@PI	Value pi (p = 3.14159265)
@PMT			@PMT	Necessary installments to pay a loan
POWER(m,n)	X	X		M to the nth power
@PROPER			@PROPER	Converts the first character of each word of a string to uppercase and returns the remaining characters in lowercase
@PV			@PV	Current value of a series of equal payments
@QUARTER			@QUARTER	Number that represents the quarter
@QUARTERBEG			@QUARTERBEG	First day of the quarter
QUOTENAME	X			A Unicode string with delimiters added to make the input string valid for SQL Server
RADIANS	X			The value in radians corresponding to the degrees specified as argument
RAISERROR	X			An error message defined by the user

Name	SQL Server 7	Oracle	SQLBase	Returns/Executes
RAND	X			A number of random float type between 0 and 1
@RATE			@RATE	Interest rate necessary to make an investment increase to a future value
RAWTOHEX		X		The argument of raw type converted to hexadecimal
READTEXT	X			Reads values of texttext, ntext, or image values
REFTOHEX		X		The argument converted from ref to hexadecimal
@REPEAT			@REPEAT	Concatenates a string with itself a certain number of times
@REPLACE			@REPLACE	Replaces characters in a string
REPLICATE	X			Replaces all the occurrences of the second argument contained in the first argument with the contents of the third argument
REVERSE	X			The inverse of a character expression
RIGHT	X	X	@RIGHT	Rightmost substring
ROUND	X	X	@ROUND	Rounds a number to the decimal places specified
ROWIDTOCHAR		X		Converts the value of type rowid to varchar2
RPAD(char1, n [,char2])		X		Char1 with the size of char2 and filled with blanks at right
RTRIM	X	X		Removes the final blanks of the argument
@SCAN			@SCAN	Looks for a standard in a string
@SDV			@SDV	Standard deviation

Name	SQL Server 7	Oracle	SQLBase	Returns/Executes
@SECOND			@SECOND	Seconds of the minute
SESSION_USER	X			Inserts a value supressed by the system for the insertion of the user's name
SIGN	X	X		-1 when the function is smaller than 0, 1 when it is greater than 0, and 0 when it is equal to zero
SIN	X	X	@SIN	Sine
SINH		X	@SIN	Hyperbolic sine
@SLN			@SLN	Linear depreciation
SOUNDEX	X	X		Returns a code of four characters to evaluate the similarity between two strings
SPACE	X			A string with the indicated number of spaces
SQRT	X	X	@SQRT	The square root
SQUARE	X			The square of the expression
STATS_DATE	X			The date on which the statistical information of the index was last updated
STDDEV		X		The standard deviation
STDEV	X			The standard deviation
STDEVP	X			The statistical standard deviation
STR	X			Data containing characters converted from numeric data
@STRING			@STRING	Converts a number into a string
STUFF	X			Deletes characters in the first expression and inserts characters from the second expression in its place

Functions ■ 197

Name	SQL Server 7	Oracle	SQLBase	Returns/Executes
SUBSTRB(char, m [,n])		X		The same as SUBSTRING, but the arguments are specified in bytes instead of characters
SUBSTRING	X	X	@SUBSTRING	Returns part of the string
SUM	X	X	X	The sum of the arguments
SUSER_NAME	X			The user's identification name
SUSER_NAME	X			The login identification name
SUSER_SID	X			The security identification number
@SYD			@SYD	Method of depreciation using the sum of the years method
SYSDATE		X		System's current date and hour
SYSTEM_USER	X			User's identification name
TAN	X	X	@TAN	Tangent (angle expressed in radians)
TANH		X		Hyperbolic tangent
@TERM			@TERM	Number of periods for the payment of an investment
TEXTPTR	X			The text pointer value in the format varbinary
TEXTVALID	X			True when a text pointer is valid
@TIME			@TIME	Returns a value of type date/hour data hour, minute, and second
@TIMEVALUE			@TIMEVALUE	Returns a value of type date/hour data HH:MM:SS [AM or PM]
TO_CHAR		X		Converts a date or number into a variable varchar2
TO_DATE		X		Converts a string into a value of data type

Name	SQL Server 7	Oracle	SQLBase	Returns/Executes
TO_MULTI_BYTE		X		The argument with all the single-byte characters converted to multi-byte
TO_NUMBER		X		Converts the argument into the type of number specified
TRANSLATE(char, from, to)		X		Returns char with all the occurrences of each character contained in the argument of the lowercase FROM clause by the arguments in the TO clause
TRANSLATE(text USING {CHAR_CS | NCHAR_CS })		X		Converts the text to the character set specified
TRIGGER_NEXTLEVEL	X			The number of triggers executed to the update, insert, or delete instruction that started the trigger
@TRIM			@TRIM	Removes blanks
TRUNC(n[,m])		X		Returns truncated n to m decimal places
TYPEPROPERTY	X			Information on a property of type data
UID		X		A unique integer number to identify the user
UNICODE	X			The Unicode value for the first byte of the expression
UPPER	X	X	@UPPER	Lowercase to uppercase
USER	X	X		Returns a string with the user identification
USER_ID	X			The identification number of the user's database
USER_NAME	X			The specified user's name

Name	SQL Server 7	Oracle	SQLBase	Returns/Executes
USERENV		X		A varchar2 variable about the current session
@VALUE			@VALUE	Converts a string of characters containing digits for a number
VAR	X			The statistical variance of the values in the list of arguments
VARIANCE		X		The variance of the argument
VARP	X			The statistical variance of the population of all the values in the list of arguments
VSIZE		X		The number of bytes of the argument representation
@WEEKBEG			@WEEKBEG	First day of the week (Monday)
@WEEKDAY			@WEEKDAY	Day of the week
YEAR	X		@YEAR	The year, based on 1900
@YEARBEG		X	@YEARBEG	First day of the year
@YEARNO			@YEARNO	Calendar year

Appendix B
Commands

This appendix contains a summary of commands and declarations supported by the SQL Server 7, Oracle 8, and SQLBase 7 databases. Many commands have the same name and function identically in more than one of the SQL dialects.

Name	SQLServer	Oracle	SQLBase	Description
ALTER CLUSTER		X		Redefines the storage and parallelism characteristics of a cluster
ALTER DATABASE	X	X	X	Changes the characteristics or log of a database
ALTER DBAREA			X	Changes the size of the database area
ALTER EXTERNAL FUNCTION			X	Changes the definition of an external function
ALTER FUNCTION		X		Recompiles an autonomous stored function
ALTER INDEX		X		Changes, reconstructs, or renames an index
ALTER PACKAGE		X		Recompiles a previously created package
ALTER PASSWORD			X	Changes the password

Name	SQLServer	Oracle	SQLBase	Description
ALTER PROCEDURE	X	X		Changes a previously created stored procedure
ALTER PROFILE		X		Changes or adds a limit to a profile
ALTER RESOURCE COST		X		Specifies the formula to calculate the cost of a session
ALTER ROLE		X		Changes the necessary permission to access a role
ALTER ROLLBACK SEGMENT		X		Changes the characteristics of a rollback segment
ALTER SEQUENCE		X		Redefines the value generated to a sequence
ALTER SNAPSHOT		X		Changes the storage characteristics of a snapshot
ALTER SNAPSHOT LOG		X		Changes the storage characteristics of a snapshot log
ALTER STOGROUP			X	Adds or deletes an area of the database for a storage group
ALTER TABLE	X	X	X	Changes the definition of a table
ALTER TABLESPACE		X		Changes the storage characteristics of a tablespace
ALTER TRIGGER	X	X	X	Enables and disables triggers defined in tables
ALTER TYPE		X		Changes or creates a user-defined type
ALTER USER		X		Changes the password or other characteristics of a user
ALTER VIEW	X	X		Changes the previously created view
ANALYZE		X		Collects statistical information about an index, table, or cluster
AUDIT MESSAGE			X	Writes a message in an audit file
BACKUP	X			Makes a backup copy of the database

Name	SQLServer	Oracle	SQLBase	Description
BEGIN DISTRIBUTED TRANSACTION	X			Specifies the beginning of a transaction, managed by the Microsoft Distributed Transaction Coordinator (MS DTC)
BEGIN...END	X	X	X	Groups a series of instructions
BEGIN TRANSACTION	X	X	X	Marks the beginning of a local transaction
BREAK	X	X	X	Quits an inner WHILE loop
BULK INSERT	X			Copies a data file to a table in a user-defined format
CASE	X			Evaluates a list of conditions
CHECK DATABASE			X	Checks the database's integrity
CHECK INDEX			X	Checks the integrity of a certain index
CHECK TABLE			X	Checks the integrity of a certain table
COMMENT		X		Adds a comment about a table to the data dictionary
COMMENT ON			X	Replaces or adds a comment to the definition of a table, view, column, or external function of the system catalog
COMMIT [transaction]	X	X	X	Terminates a logical work unit and makes its changes in the database
CONTINUE	X	X	X	Reinitializes a WHILE loop
CREATE CLUSTER		X		Creates a cluster
CREATE DATABASE	X	X	X	Physically creates a database
CREATE DBAREA			X	Creates a database area
CREATE DEFAULT	X			Creates a default object
CREATE DIRECTORY		X		Creates a directory object, which represents a directory of the operating system to administrate the access to the BFILEs stored outside of the database

Name	SQLServer	Oracle	SQLBase	Description
CREATE EVENT			X	Creates an event
CREATE EXTERNAL FUNCTION			X	Creates an external function
CREATE FUNCTION		X		Creates a user-defined function
CREATE INDEX	X	X	X	Creates an index in a table
CREATE LIBRARY		X		Creates an object that represents a DLL library of the system
CREATE PACKAGE		X		Creates a package of procedures and functions
CREATE PACKAGE BODY		X		Creates the body of a package
CREATE PROCEDURE	X	X		Creates a stored procedure
CREATE PROFILE		X		Creates a profile, which is a set of limits for the database
CREATE ROLE		X		Creates a role
CREATE ROLLBACK SEGMENT		X		Creates a rollback segment
CREATE RULE	X			Creates a rule object
CREATE SCHEMA	X			Creates a database schema
CREATE SEQUENCE		X		Creates a sequence of numbers
CREATE SNAPSHOT		X		Creates a snapshot (result of a query)
CREATE SNAPSHOT LOG		X		Creates a snapshot log
CREATE STOGROUP			X	Creates a storage group
CREATE SYNONYM		X	X	Defines an alternate name for a table, view, or external function
CREATE TABLE	X	X	X	Creates a table
CREATE TABLESPACE		X		Creates a tablespace

Name	SQLServer	Oracle	SQLBase	Description
CREATE TRIGGER	X	X	X	Creates a trigger
CREATE TYPE		X		Creates an object type
CREATE TYPE BODY		X		Creates the methods to define an object type
CREATE USER		X		Creates a database user
CREATE VIEW	X	X	X	Creates a database view
DBATTRIBUTE			X	Configures specific attributes of the database
DEALLOCATE	X			Removes the reference to a cursor
DECLARE CURSOR	X			Defines the attributes of a cursor
DEINSTALL DATABASE			X	Removes a database from the network, making it unavailable to the users
DELETE	X	X	X	Deletes one or more rows of a table
DENY	X			Creates access restrictions to the database
DROP CURSOR		X		Removes a cursor
DROP DATABASE	X		X	Physically deletes a database
DROP DATABASE LINK		X		Removes a database link
DROP DBAREA			X	Physically deletes an area of the database
DROP DEFAULT	X			Removes one or more user-defined defaults
DROP DIRECTORY		X		Removes a directory object
DROP EVENT			X	Deletes an event
DROP EXTERNAL FUNCTION			X	Deletes an external function
DROP FUNCTION		X		Removes a function

Name	SQLServer	Oracle	SQLBase	Description
DROP INDEX	X	X	X	Removes an index
DROP LIBRARY		X		Removes the system library
DROP PACKAGE		X		Removes a package of procedures and functions
DROP PROCEDURE	X	X		Removes a stored procedure
DROP PROFILE		X		Removes a profile
DROP ROLE		X		Removes a role
DROP ROLLBACK SEGMENT		X		Removes a rollback segment
DROP RULE	X			Removes a user-defined rule
DROP SEQUENCE		X		Removes a sequence
DROP STOGROUP			X	Deletes a storage group
DROP SNAPSHOT		X		Removes a snapshot
DROP SNAPSHOT LOG		X		Removes the log file of a snaphot
DROP STATISTICS	X			Deletes statistical information from a column in a table
DROP SYNONYM			X	Deletes a synonym
DROP TABLE	X	X	X	Physically deletes a table from a database
DROP TABLESPACE		X		Removes the database's tablespace
DROP TRIGGER	X	X	X	Deletes a trigger
DROP VIEW	X	X	X	Deletes a view
DUMP	X			Creates a backup copy of the database
ELSE	X	X	X	Enforces execution conditions for an IF command
EXECUTE	X			Executes a procedure

Name	SQLServer	Oracle	SQLBase	Description
EXISTS	X	X	X	Specifies a subquery to test the existence of rows
EXPLAIN PLAN		X		Creates an execution plan for a query
FETCH	X			Restores the specific row of a cursor
FROM	X	X	X	Specifies the origin of tables and views used in the SELECT, INSERT, and UPDATE commands
GRANT (database authority)	X	X	X	Marks authorization or privilege levels for a database
GRANT (table privileges)			X	Marks one or more specific privileges for a table or view
GRANT EXECUTE ON			X	Marks privilege to users for the execution of stored procedures and external functions
IF..ELSE	X	X	X	Evaluates a conditional expression and executes another specified command
INSERT	X	X	X	Inserts one or more rows in an existing table
INSTALL DATABASE			X	Puts the database in the network, making it available to users
KILL	X			Terminates the user process
LABEL			X	Adds or changes labels in the catalog definitions
LOAD			X	Loads one or more tables in a database
LOCK DATABASE			X	Puts an exclusive lock on the database, preventing connections by other users
OPEN	X			Opens a cursor and executes the SQL-specified interaction
PRINT	X			Returns a user-defined message
PROCEDURE			X	Creates a procedure

Name	SQLServer	Oracle	SQLBase	Description
RENAME		X		Renames a table
RESTORE	X			Restores the database from a backup file
REVOKE	X	X	X	Removes authorization or privilege levels from a database
REVOKE EXECUTE ON			X	Removes user privilege for the execution of stored procedures and external functions
ROLLBACK	X	X	X	Terminates the logical work unit and undoes the changes made to the database during the last transaction
ROWCOUNT			X	Counts the number of rows in a table
SAVE TRANSACTION	X			Marks a savepoint inside a transaction
SAVEPOINT		X	X	Determines a checkpoint inside a transaction
SELECT	X	X	X	Chooses rows in tables or views
SET CONSTRAINTS		X		Specifies a transaction when a constraint is checked during a DML command
SET DEFAULT STOGROUP			X	Specifies a default storage group
SET TRANSACTION		X		Adjusts the characteristics of a transaction
START AUDIT			X	Initiates a database audit
STOP AUDIT			X	Terminates a database audit
TRUNCATE TABLE	X			Eliminates all the rows of a table
UNION	X	X	X	Combines results from two or more queries in one set of results
UNLOAD			X	Downloads the database to an external file

Name	SQLServer	Oracle	SQLBase	Description
UNLOCK DATABASE			X	Frees the exclusive lock of a database
UPDATE	X	X	X	Updates the values of columns in a table or view
UPDATE STATISTICS	X		X	Updates the statistics of an index in a table
UPDATETEXT	X			Updates a field of type text, ntext, or image
WAITFOR	X			Specifies the hour in which an event triggers a procedure or transaction
WHERE	X	X	X	Filters a query to the database
WHILE	X			Establishes a condition for the repetitive execution of a block of SQL commands
WRITETEXT	X			Allows the update of a column of type text, ntext, or image, overriding previous contents

Appendix C
Data Types

Each column in a table is required to contain a specific type of data. In other words, it is necessary to indicate whether the column will store text, number, data, image, or another type of data. The following table shows the data types supported by the SQL Server 7, Oracle 8, and SQLBase 7 databases.

Data Type	SQL Server 7	Oracle 8	SQLBase
Bfile		X	
Binary	X		
Bit	X		
Blob		X	
Char	X	X	X
Clob		X	
Cursor	X		
Date		X	X
Datetime	X		X
Decimal	X		X
Double Precision			X

Appendix C

Data Type	SQL Server 7	Oracle 8	SQLBase
Float	X		X
Image	X		
Integer or Int	X		X
Long		X	X
Long Raw		X	
Long Varchar			X
Mlslabel		X	
Money	X		
Nchar	X	X	
Nclob		X	
Ntext	X		
Number		X	X
Numeric	X		
Nvarchar	X		
Nvarchar2		X	
Raw		X	
Real	X		X
Rowid		X	
Smalldatetime	X		
Smallint	X		X
Smallmoney	X		
Text	X		
Time			X
Timestamp	X		X
Tinyint	X		

Data Type	SQL Server 7	Oracle 8	SQLBase
Uniqueidentifier	X		
Varbinary	X		
Varchar	X		X
Varchar2		X	

The following sections outline the unique characteristics of each database's data types.

SQL Server 7

SQL Server 7 supports many data types and also allows the user to create his or her own. Below is a list of the SQL Server 7 data types.

Data Type	Description
Binary	Fixed size of up to 8,000 bytes
Bit	Integer with a value of 0 or 1
Char	Fixed field with maximum size of 8,000 bytes
Cursor	A reference to a cursor
Datetime	January 1, 1753, to December 31, 9999, with precision of 3.3 milliseconds
Decimal and numeric	Fixed precision from $-10^{38} -1$ to $10^{38} -1$
Float	$-1.79E + 308$ to $1.79E + 308$
Image	Variable size with up to $2^{31} - 1$ (2,147,483,647) bytes
Int	Integer number with values from -2^{31} ($-2,147,483,648$) to $2^{31} - 1$ (2,147,483,647)
Money	Monetary values from 2^{63} ($-922,337,203,685,477.5808$) up to $2^{63} - 1$ ($+922,337,203,685,477.5807$)
Nchar	Unicode character of fixed size up to 4,000 bytes
Ntext	Variable with size from $2^{30} - 1$ (1,073,741,823) bytes
Nvarchar	Unicode character with variable size of up to 4,000 bytes
Real	$-3.40E + 38$ to $3.40E + 38$

Smalldatetime	January 1, 1900, to June 6, 2079, with precision of 1 minute
Smallint	2^15 (–32,768) to 2^15 – 1 (32,767)
Smallmoney	–214,748.3648 to +214,748.3647
Text	Variable with size of up to 2^31 – 1 (2,147,483,647) bytes
Timestamp	A unique number recognized by the database
Tinyint	Integer between 0 and 255
Uniqueidentifier	A unique global identifier
Varbinary	Variable size of up to 8,000 bytes
Varchar	Fixed field with maximum size of 8,000 bytes

Synonyms

There are several synonyms created for compatibility between SQL Server 7 and SQL-92:

ANSI SQL Data Type	SQL Server 7 Data Type
binary varying	varbinary
char varying	varchar
character	char
character	char(1)
character(n)	char(n)
character varying(n)	varchar(n)
dec	decimal
double precision	float
float[(n)] for n = 1-7	real
float[(n)] for n = 8-15	float

ANSI SQL Data Type	SQL Server 7 Data Type
integer	int
national character(n)	nchar(n)
national char(n)	nchar(n)
national character varying(n)	nvarchar(n)
national char varying(n)	nvarchar(n)
national text	ntext
numeric	decimal

Oracle 8

Oracle 8 also has several standard data types and allows the user to create his or her own data types. Below are the data types supported by Oracle.

Data Type	Description
Bfile	Contains a locator to an external binary file; the maximum size is 4 Gbytes
Blob	A binary object with maximum size of 4 Gbytes
Char(size)	Fixed field with maximum size of 2,000 bytes
Clob	A binary object containing characters of single-byte type; the maximum size is 4 Gbytes
Date	Valid date from Jan. 1, 4712 B.C. to Dec. 31, 4712
Long	Variable character with size of up to 2 Gbytes
Long Raw	Variable of type raw binary with size of up to 2 Gbytes
Mlslabel	Binary format with a label of the operating system; currently not used
Nchar(size)	Data of fixed size and character type with maximum size of 2,000 bytes
Nclob	Object of character type containing characters of multi-byte type with a fixed size of up to 4 Gbytes
Nvarchar2(size)	Data of character type with variable size limited to 4,000 bytes

Number(p,s)
: Data of number type with precision p and scale s; the precision can vary from 1 to 38 and the scale from –84 to +127

Raw(size)
: Data of raw binary type with maximum size of 2000 bytes

Rowid
: String hexadecimal representing the unique address of a table row

Varchar2(size)
: Data of character type with variable size and limited to 4,000 bytes

Synonyms

Some synonyms were created for compatibility between Oracle 8 and the SQL-92 language:

ANSI SQL Data Type	Oracle Data Type
CHARACTER(n) CHAR(n)	CHAR(n)
CHARACTER VARYING(n) CHAR VARYING(n)	VARCHAR(n)
NATIONAL CHARACTER(n) NATIONAL CHAR(n) NCHAR(n)	NCHAR(n)
NATIONAL CHARACTER VARYING(n) NATIONAL CHAR VARYING(n) NCHAR VARYING(n)	NVARCHAR2(n)
NUMERIC(p,s) DECIMAL(p,s)	NUMBER(p,s)
INTEGER INT SMALLINT	NUMBER(38)

ANSI SQL Data Type	Oracle Data Type
FLOAT(b) DOUBLE PRECISION REAL	NUMBER

SQLBase

Next is a summary of the characteristics of data types supported by SQLBase.

Data Type	Description
Char	Data of character type with fixed size of up to 254 characters
Date	Stores only the date
Datetime or Timestamp	When part of the input argument is omitted, SQLBase assumes the default 0 that converts the date to 30/12/1899, and 12:00 a.m.
Decimal or Dec	Supports up to 15 digits (−999999999999999 to +999999999999999); when not specified, assumes precision 5 and scale 0
Double Precision	Numeric data of type floating-point with double precision
Float	When the precision is specified between 1 and 21, the data type will have single precision; between 22 and 53 it will have double precision
Integer or Int	Data of type integer can have up to 10 digits of precision (−2147483648 to +2147483647)
Long Varchar	Stores characters or binary objects; equivalent to data of type blob
Number	This is a superset of other data types; it supports precision of up to 22 digits
Real	Numeric data of type floating-point with single precision

Smallint   This data type truncates the digits to the right of the decimal point and can have up to five digits of precision (−32,768 to +32,767)

Time   Stores only the hour

Varchar   Data of character type with fixed size of up to 254 characters

Appendix D
Installing Centura SQLBase 7

This appendix shows how to install the 60-day evaluation copy of the Centura SQLBase 7 database included on the companion CD. This copy is a complete version of the product, but expires 60 days from the installation date.

Insert the CD-ROM in the appropriate drive. Double-click on the drive and open the SQLBase folder. Double-click on setup.exe. Press the Next button in the first screen.

The second screen warns about the 60-day limit on the software.

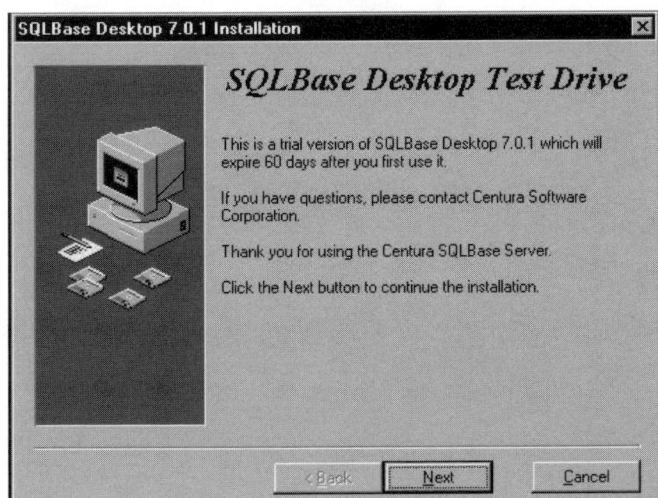

After you press Next, the program shows the license agreement. If you agree, press Next. The program then asks you to choose whether you want the express or customized installation. Keep the option Express selected, as shown below, and press Next.

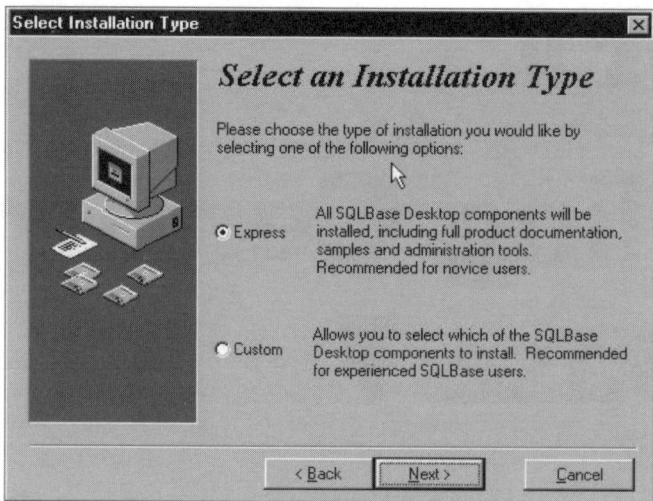

In the next step, either confirm the given folder for the installation or enter another folder. In this example we have changed the installation drive to e:. You can also press the Browse button and select another directory.

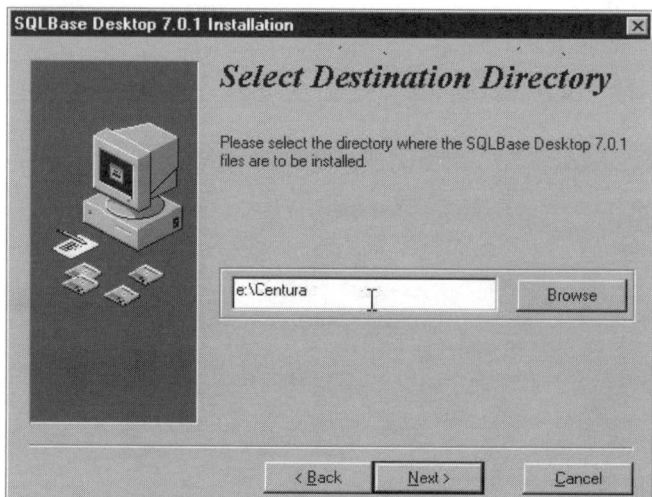

Installing Centura SQLBase 7 ■ 221

The program then asks you to confirm the creation of the program group. Press Next to confirm or change the name of the program group. Then press Next to start the installation. The process is initiated and in a few seconds the program will be installed.

In the next screen that appears, press Finish. You will have to restart the computer for the changes to take effect.

After you restart your computer, a screen shows the items that were installed, using a display similar to that shown below.

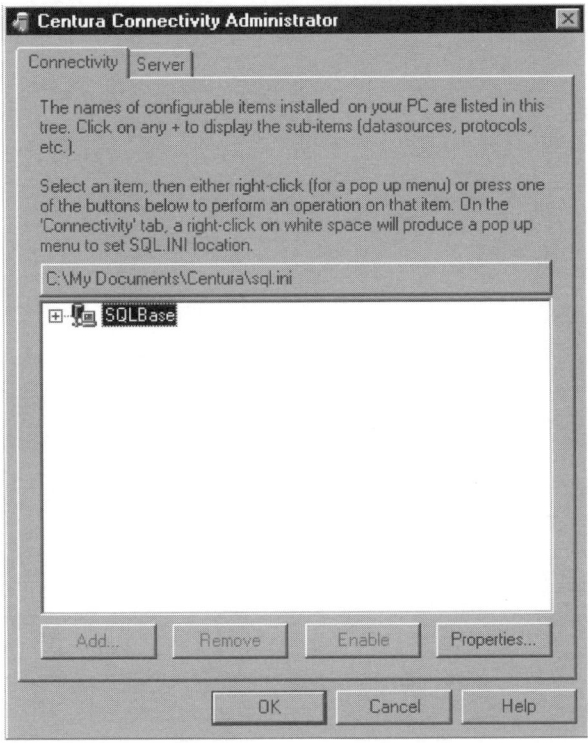

Press the plus sign to see the items that were installed and then press OK to continue.

Appendix E
The Example Database

This appendix contains instructions for installing the Pubssqlb database. Use this database to follow the examples and practice what you have learned.

On the companion CD there is a directory called Demosql. In it you will find some files that must be copied to your hard disk. First you must create a Pubssqlb folder in the Centura folder. Using Windows Explorer, click and drag the pubssqlb.dbs file from the Demosql folder to the Pubssqlb folder.

After copying the file, open the Connectivity Administrator program by clicking on Start|Programs|Centura|SQLBase Desktop 7.0.1|Connectivity Administrator.

Select the Server tab and click on the plus sign next to the server name to expand the tree. Expand the Listening Protocols and Databases items. Check to see if Local Connection is below Listening Protocols.

224 ■ Appendix E

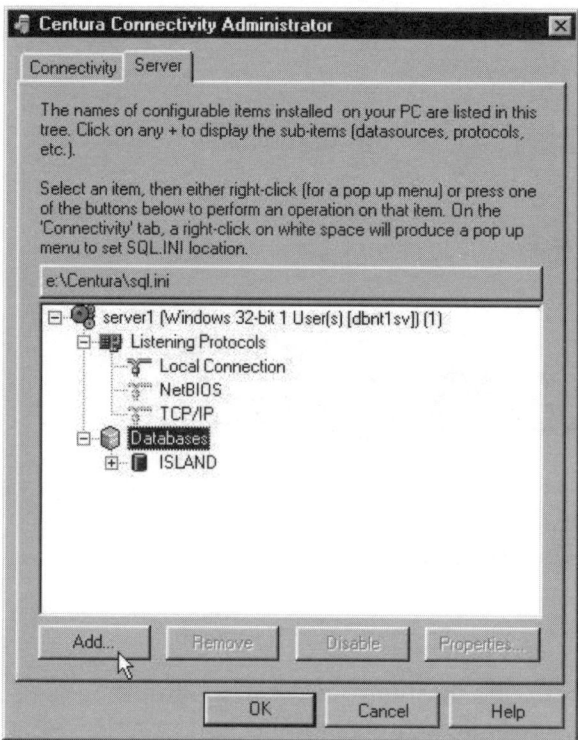

Select Databases and press Add. The following screen appears.

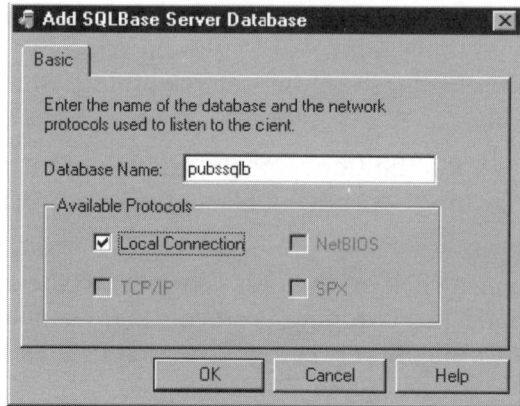

Enter the name of the database, pubssqlb in this example, and check the Local Connection box. Press OK.

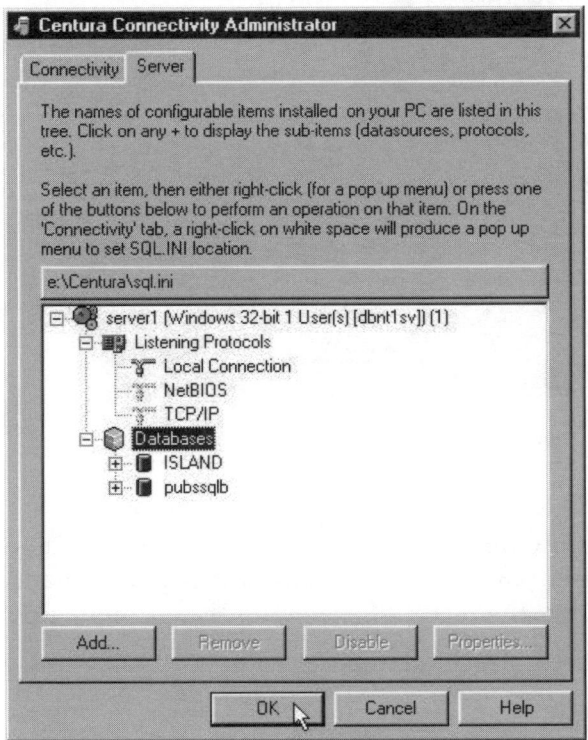

The new database appears in the list of databases.

Press the OK button to finish. A message warns that changes will take effect the next time the database is loaded. Press OK.

Open the SQLBase Database Engine by clicking on Start|Programs|Centura|SQLBase Desktop 7.0.1|SQLBase Database Engine. Press OK in the screen that appears. Then select Display from the menu bar and the Databases option to display the available databases. Both the Island and Pubssqlb databases will appear in the list.

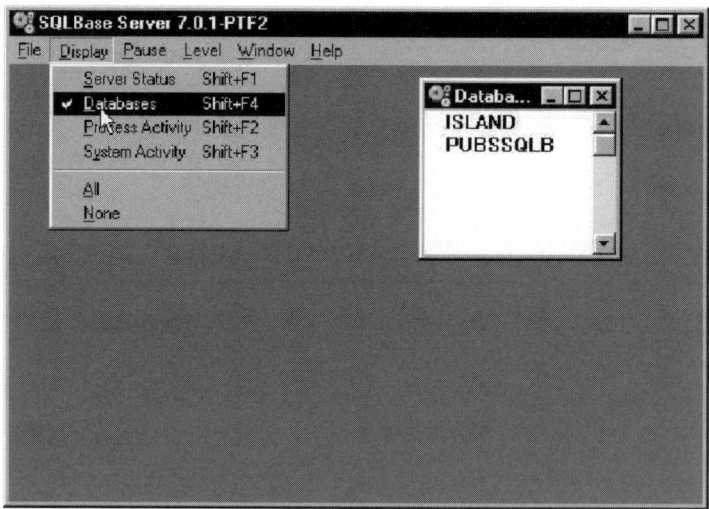

Connecting to the Database

Open SQLTalk by clicking on Start|Programs|Centura|SQLBase Desktop 7.0.1|SQLTalk Interactive SQL 32bit. The working screen contains two panels. The upper panel is used to enter the SQL commands, and the lower panel shows the result of executing these commands.

To connect to the Pubssqlb database, enter:

Connect pubssqlb;

and press the Ctrl+Enter keys. Note that in SQLTalk every line must end with a semicolon.

After the command is executed, a message appears that says the connection with the database was established as shown below.

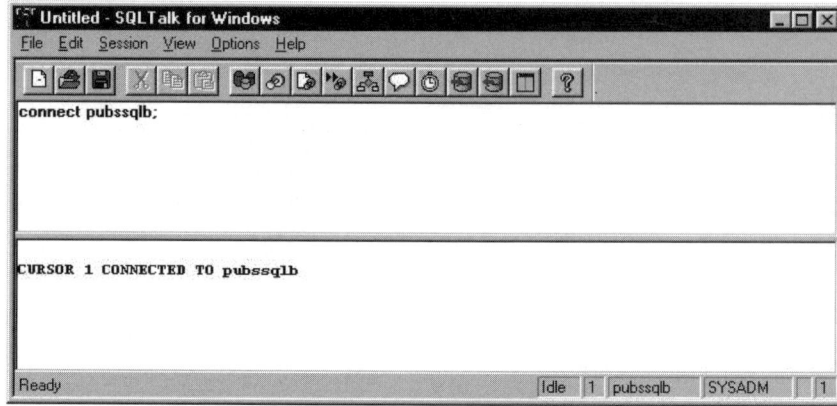

Executing SQL Commands

After you are connected to the database, all the tables and objects in the database are available. Now you can execute any SQL command on the database.

Here are some basic rules for executing commands:

1. Every command line must end with a semicolon (;).
2. To execute the command entered, the cursor must be positioned in the line of that command.
3. Commands can be executed in several ways. You can press the keys Ctrl+Enter simultaneously; press the keys Shift+F2; or position the cursor in the command line and press the Execute button.

The next figure shows the results of a simple query being displayed in the lower panel.

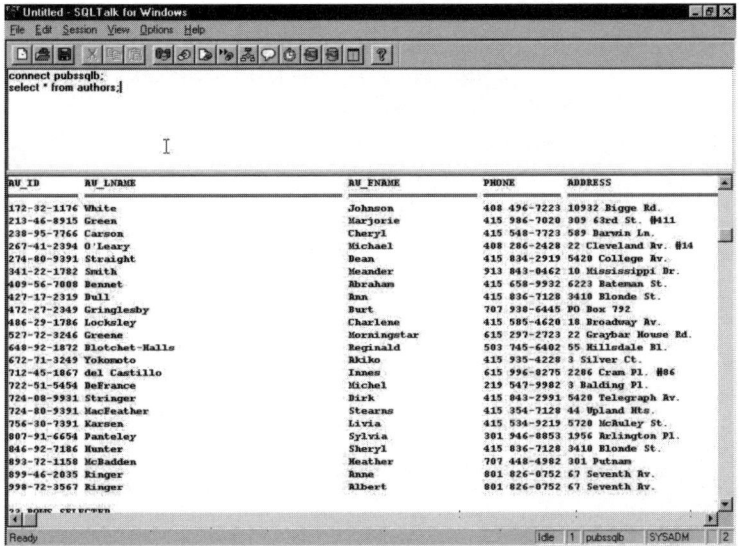

You can have several lines of commands in the upper panel. Only the line where the vertical cursor is positioned will be executed.

The Button Bar

Several tasks can be performed using the button bar. These are summarized, from left to right, below.

New	Clears the command area and allows the entry of new commands. All the connections with databases are active.
Open	Opens a previously written command file.
Save	Saves the commands to the command area in a file for further execution.
Cut	Deletes the selected command and places the rows and columns of the result area on the clipboard.
Copy	Copies the current selection to the clipboard.
Paste	Places contents from the clipboard at the insertion point.
Connect	Opens the database connection dialog box.
Execute Command	Executes the current command.
Execute Script	Executes the selected script file.
View Last Command	Displays the last command that was executed.
View Execute Plan	Switches between the result view and execution panel.
Verbose Messages	Allows you to toggle to receive more detailed error messages.
Toggle Command Timer	Displays/hides the time necessary to obtain the result of a certain SQL command.
Commit	Writes changes to the database.
Rollback	Undoes the changes made to the database. When Rollback is not active, just the current command is undone.

Change Split	Changes the vertical panels to horizontal, and vice versa.
Help	Accesses the help files.

Installing the Executable Program

On the CD you will find an application showing the use of the SQL language embedded inside another language. In this example, created by Ana Paula Bonani of Centura Brasil, an application in Centura accesses the Pubssqlb database.

Click on the Deploy15.exe item in the Demosql directory on the companion CD. The following screen appears.

Press the Next button.

In the second screen choose the directory where SQLBase was installed. If it was installed in the default directory, simply press Next. Otherwise, press the Browse button and select the desired directory.

The next screen announces that the installation will begin. Press Next to start the process of copying the files.

When the file copy operation is complete, the program asks you to press the Finish button.

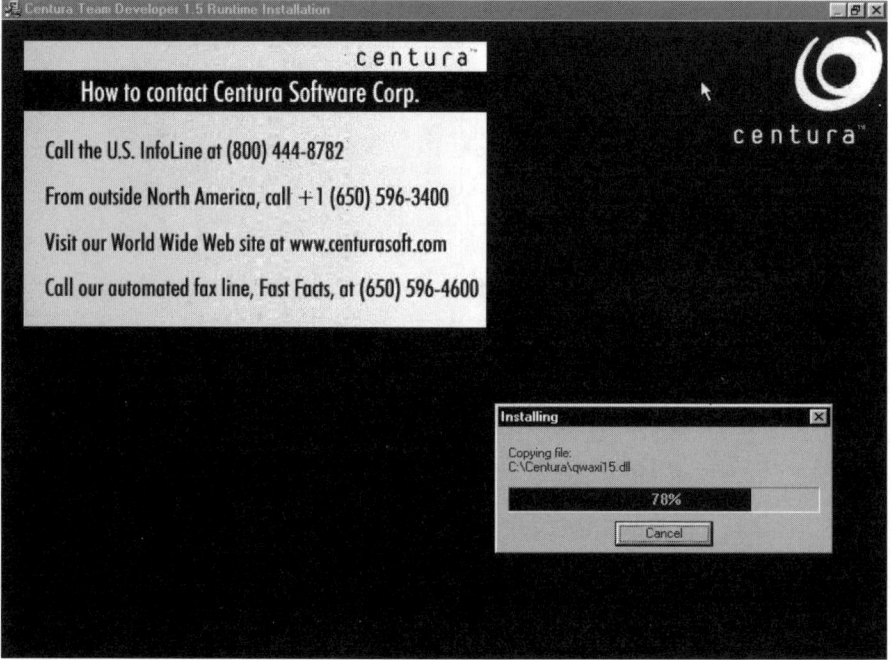

Now you must copy the executable program of the application to the directory where Centura was installed. Bookstore.exe can also be found in the Demosql directory.

Appendix F
Structure and Contents of Tables

This appendix shows the structure of most of the tables in the Pubssqlb database, as well as their contents. These are included to help you follow the examples throughout the book.

The PUBLISHERS Table

Structure:

NAME	TBNAME	TBCREATOR	COLNO	COLTYPE	LENGTH	SCALE	NULLS
PUB_ID	PUBLISHERS	SYSADM	1	CHAR	4	0	N
PUB_NAME	PUBLISHERS	SYSADM	2	VARCHAR	40	0	Y
CITY	PUBLISHERS	SYSADM	3	VARCHAR	20	0	Y
STATE	PUBLISHERS	SYSADM	4	CHAR	2	0	Y
COUNTRY	PUBLISHERS	SYSADM	5	VARCHAR	30	0	Y

Contents:

PUB_ID	PUB_NAME	CITY	STATE	COUNTRY
0736	New Moon Books	Boston	MA	USA
0877	Binnet & Hardley	Washington	DC	USA
1389	Algodata Infosystems	Berkeley	CA	USA
1622	Five Lakes Publishing	Chicago	IL	USA

1756	Ramona Publishers	Dallas	TX	USA
9901	GGG&G	Munchen		Germany
9952	Scootney Books	New York	NY	USA
9999	Lucerne Publishing	Paris		France

The SALES Table

Structure:

NAME	TBNAME	TBCREATOR	COLNO	COLTYPE	LENGTH	SCALE	NULLS
STOR_ID	SALES	SYSADM	1	CHAR	4	0	N
ORD_NUM	SALES	SYSADM	2	VARCHAR	20	0	N
ORD_DATE	SALES	SYSADM	3	TIMESTMP	10	0	N
QTY	SALES	SYSADM	4	SMALLINT	2	0	N
PAYTERMS	SALES	SYSADM	5	VARCHAR	12	0	N
TITLE_ID	SALES	SYSADM	6	VARCHAR	6	0	Y

Contents:

STOR_ID	ORD_NUM	ORD_DATE	QTY	PAYTERMS	TITLE_ID
6380	6871	14-SEP-1994 00:00:00	5	Net 60	BU1032
6380	722a	13-SEP-1994 00:00:00	3	Net 60	PS2091
7066	A2976	24-MAY-1993 00:00:00	50	Net 30	PC8888
7066	QA7442.3	13-SEP-1994 00:00:00	75	ON invoice	PS2091
7067	D4482	14-SEP-1994 00:00:00	10	Net 60	PS2091
7067	P2121	15-JUN-1992 00:00:00	40	Net 30	TC3218
7067	P2121	15-JUN-1992 00:00:00	20	Net 30	TC4203
7067	P2121	15-JUN-1992 00:00:00	20	Net 30	TC7777
7131	N914008	14-SEP-1994 00:00:00	20	Net 30	PS2091
7131	N914014	14-SEP-1994 00:00:00	25	Net 30	MC3021
7131	P3087a	29-MAY-1993 00:00:00	20	Net 60	PS1372
7131	P3087a	29-MAY-1993 00:00:00	25	Net 60	PS2106
7131	P3087a	29-MAY-1993 00:00:00	15	Net 60	PS3333
7131	P3087a	29-MAY-1993 00:00:00	25	Net 60	PS7777
7896	QQ2299	28-OCT-1993 00:00:00	15	Net 60	BU7832
7896	TQ456	12-DEC-1993 00:00:00	10	Net 60	MC2222
7896	X999	21-FEB-1993 00:00:00	35	On invoice	BU2075
8042	423LL922	14-SEP-1994 00:00:00	15	On invoice	MC3021
8042	423LL930	14-SEP-1994 00:00:00	10	On invoice	BU1032
8042	P723	11-MAR-1993 00:00:00	25	Net 30	BU1111
8042	QA879.1	22-MAY-1993 00:00:00	30	Net 30	PC1035

The AUTHORS Table

Structure:

NAME	TBNAME	TBCREATOR	COLNO	COLTYPE	LENGTH	SCALE	NULLS
AU_ID	AUTHORS	SYSADM	1	VARCHAR	11	0	Y
AU_LNAME	AUTHORS	SYSADM	2	VARCHAR	40	0	N
AU_FNAME	AUTHORS	SYSADM	3	VARCHAR	20	0	N
PHONE	AUTHORS	SYSADM	4	CHAR	12	0	N
ADDRESS	AUTHORS	SYSADM	5	VARCHAR	40	0	Y
CITY	AUTHORS	SYSADM	6	VARCHAR	20	0	Y
STATE	AUTHORS	SYSADM	7	CHAR	2	0	Y
ZIP	AUTHORS	SYSADM	8	CHAR	5	0	Y
CONTRACT	AUTHORS	SYSADM	9	SMALLINT	2	0	Y

Contents:

AU_ID	AU_LNAME	AU_FNAME	PHONE	ADDRESS	CITY	STATE	ZIP	CONTRACT
172-32-1176	White	Johnson	408 496-7223	10932 Bigge Rd.	Menlo Park	CA	94025	1
213-46-8915	Green	Marjorie	415 986-7020	309 63rd St. #411	Oakland	CA	94618	1
238-95-7766	Carson	Cheryl	415 548-7723	589 Darwin Ln.	Berkeley	CA	94705	1
267-41-2394	O'Leary	Michael	408 286-2428	22 Cleveland Av. #14	San Jose	CA	95128	1
274-80-9391	Straight	Dean	415 834-2919	5420 College Av.	Oakland	CA	94609	1
341-22-1782	Smith	Meander	913 843-0462	10 Mississippi Dr.	Lawrence	KS	66044	0
409-56-7008	Bennet	Abraham	415 658-9932	6223 Bateman St.	Berkeley	CA	94705	1
427-17-2319	Dull	Ann	415 836-7128	3410 Blonde St.	Palo Alto	CA	94301	1
472-27-2349	Gringlesby	Burt	707 938-6445	PO Box 792	Covelo	CA	95428	1
486-29-1786	Locksley	Charlene	415 585-4620	18 Broadway Av.	San Francisco	CA	94130	1
527-72-3246	Greene	Morningstar	615 297-2723	22 Graybar House Rd.	Nashville	TN	37215	0
648-92-1872	Blotchet-Halls	Reginald	503 745-6402	55 Hillsdale Bl.	Corvallis	OR	97330	1
672-71-3249	Yokomoto	Akiko	415 935-4228	3 Silver Ct.	Walnut Creek	CA	94595	1
712-45-1867	del Castillo	Innes	615 996-8275	2286 Cram Pl. #86	Ann Arbor	MI	48105	1
722-51-5454	DeFrance	Michel	219 547-9982	3 Balding Pl.	Gary	IN	46403	1
724-08-9931	Stringer	Dirk	415 843-2991	5420 Telegraph Ave.	Oakland	CA	94609	0
724-80-9391	MacFeather	Stearns	415 354-7128	44 Upland Hts.	Oakland	CA	94612	1
756-30-7391	Karsen	Livia	415 534-9219	5720 McAuley St.	Oakland	CA	94609	1
807-91-6654	Panteley	Sylvia	301 946-8853	1956 Arlington Pl.	Rockville	MD	20853	1
846-92-7186	Hunter	Sheryl	415 836-7128	3410 Blonde St.	Palo Alto	CA	94301	1
893-72-1158	McBadden	Heather	707 448-4982	301 Putnam	Vacaville	CA	95688	0
899-46-2035	Ringer	Anne	801 826-0752	67 Seventh Av.	Salt Lake City	UT	84152	1
998-72-3567	Ringer	Albert	801 826-0752	67 Seventh Av.	Salt Lake City	UT	84152	1

The TITLEAUTHOR Table

Structure:

NAME	TBNAME	TBCREATOR	COLNO	COLTYPE	LENGTH	SCALE	NULLS
AU_ID	TITLEAUTHOR	SYSADM	1	VARCHAR	11	0	Y
TITLE_ID	TITLEAUTHOR	SYSADM	2	VARCHAR	6	0	Y
AU_ORD	TITLEAUTHOR	SYSADM	3	SMALLINT	2	0	Y
ROYALTYPER	TITLEAUTHOR	SYSADM	4	INTEGER	4	0	Y

Contents:

AU_ID	TITLE_ID	AU_ORD	ROYALTYPER
172-32-1176	PS3333	1	100
213-46-8915	BU1032	2	40
213-46-8915	BU2075	1	100
238-95-7766	PC1035	1	100
267-41-2394	BU1111	2	40
267-41-2394	TC7777	2	30
274-80-9391	BU7832	1	100
409-56-7008	BU1032	1	60
427-17-2319	PC8888	1	50
472-27-2349	TC7777	3	30
486-29-1786	PC9999	1	100
486-29-1786	PS7777	1	100
648-92-1872	TC4203	1	100
672-71-3249	TC7777	1	40
712-45-1867	MC2222	1	100
722-51-5454	MC3021	1	75
724-80-9391	BU1111	1	60
724-80-9391	PS1372	2	25
756-30-7391	PS1372	1	75
807-91-6654	TC3218	1	100
846-92-7186	PC8888	2	50
899-46-2035	MC3021	2	25
899-46-2035	PS2091	2	50
998-72-3567	PS2091	1	50
998-72-3567	PS2106	1	100

The STORES Table

Structure:

NAME	TBNAME	TBCREATOR	COLNO	COLTYPE	LENGTH	SCALE	NULLS
STOR_ID	STORES	SYSADM	1	CHAR	4	0	N
STOR_NAME	STORES	SYSADM	2	VARCHAR	40	0	Y
STOR_ADDRESS	STORES	SYSADM	3	VARCHAR	40	0	Y
CITY	STORES	SYSADM	4	VARCHAR	20	0	Y
STATE	STORES	SYSADM	5	CHAR	2	0	Y
ZIP	STORES	SYSADM	6	CHAR	5	0	Y

Contents:

STOR_ID	STOR_NAME	STOR_ADDRESS	CITY	STATE	ZIP
6380	Eric the Read Books	788 Catamaugus Ave.	Seattle	WA	98056
7066	Barnum's	567 Pasadena Ave.	Tustin	CA	92789
7067	News & Brews	577 First St.	Los Gatos	CA	96745
7131	Doc-U-Mat: Quality Laundry and Books	24-A Avogadro Way	Remulade	WA	98014
7896	Fricative Bookshop	89 Madison St.	Fremont	CA	90019
8042	Bookbeat	679 Carson St.	Portland	OR	89076

The JOBS Table

Structure:

NAME	TBNAME	TBCREATOR	COLNO	COLTYPE	LENGTH	SCALE	NULLS
JOB_ID	JOBS	SYSADM	1	SMALLINT	2	0	Y
JOB_DESC	JOBS	SYSADM	2	VARCHAR	50	0	N
MIN_LVL	JOBS	SYSADM	3	SMALLINT	2	0	N
MAX_LVL	JOBS	SYSADM	4	SMALLINT	2	0	N

Contents:

JOB_ID	JOB_DESC	MIN_LVL	MAX_LVL
1	New Hire - Job not specified	10	10
2	Chief Executive Officer	200	250
3	Business Operations Manager	175	225
4	Chief Financial Officer	175	250
5	Publisher	150	250
6	Managing Editor	140	225
7	Marketing Manager	120	200

Contents: (continued)

JOB_ID	JOB_DESC	MIN_LVL	MAX_LVL
8	Public Relations Manager	100	175
9	Acquisitions Manager	75	175
10	Productions Manager	75	165
11	Operations Manager	75	150
12	Editor	25	100
13	Sales Representative	25	100

The EMPLOYEE Table

Structure:

NAME	TBNAME	TBCREATOR	COLNO	COLTYPE	LENGTH	SCALE	NULLS
EMP_ID	EMPLOYEE	SYSADM	1	CHAR	9	0	Y
FNAME	EMPLOYEE	SYSADM	2	VARCHAR	20	0	N
MINIT	EMPLOYEE	SYSADM	3	CHAR	1	0	Y
LNAME	EMPLOYEE	SYSADM	4	VARCHAR	30	0	N
JOB_ID	EMPLOYEE	SYSADM	5	SMALLINT	2	0	N
JOB_LVL	EMPLOYEE	SYSADM	6	SMALLINT	2	0	N
PUB_ID	EMPLOYEE	SYSADM	7	CHAR	4	0	N
HIRE_DATE	EMPLOYEE	SYSADM	8	TIMESTMP	10	0	N

Contents:

EMP_ID	FNAME	MINIT	LNAME	JOB_ID	JOB_LVL	PUB_ID	HIRE_DATE
PMA42628M	Paolo	M	Accorti	13	35	0877	27-AUG-1992 00:00:00
PSA89086M	Pedro	S	Afonso	14	89	1389	24-DEC-1990 00:00:00
VPA30890F	Victoria	P	Ashworth	6	140	0877	13-SEP-1990 00:00:00
H-B39728F	Helen		Bennett	12	35	0877	21-SEP-1989 00:00:00
L-B31947F	Lesley		Brown	7	120	0877	13-FEB-1991 00:00:00
F-C16315M	Francisco		Chang	4	227	9952	03-NOV-1990 00:00:00
PTC11962M	Philip	T	Cramer	2	215	9952	11-NOV-1989 00:00:00
A-C71970F	Aria		Cruz	10	87	1389	26-OCT-1991 00:00:00
AMD15433F	Ann	M	Devon	3	200	9952	16-JUL-1991 00:00:00
ARD36773F	Anabela	R	Domingues	8	100	0877	27-JAN-1993 00:00:00
PHF38899M	Peter	H	Franken	10	75	0877	17-MAY-1992 00:00:00
PXH22250M	Paul	X	Henriot	5	159	0877	19-AUG-1993 00:00:00
CFH28514M	Carlos	F	Hern dez	5	211	9999	21-APR-1989 00:00:00
PDI47470M	Palle	D	Ibsen	7	195	0736	09-MAY-1993 00:00:00
KJJ92907F	Karla	J	Jablonski	9	170	9999	11-MAR-1994 00:00:00

EMP_ID	FNAME	MINIT	LNAME	JOB_ID	JOB_LVL	PUB_ID	HIRE_DATE
KFJ64308F	Karin	F	Josephs	14	100	0736	17-OCT-1992 00:00:00
MGK44605M	Matti	G	Karttunen	6	220	0736	01-MAY-1994 00:00:00
POK93028M	Pirkko	O	Koskitalo	10	80	9999	29-NOV-1993 00:00:00
JYL26161F	Janine	Y	Labrune	5	172	9901	26-MAY-1991 00:00:00
M-L67958F	Maria		Larsson	7	135	1389	27-MAR-1992 00:00:00
Y-L77953M	Yoshi		Latimer	12	32	1389	11-JUN-1989 00:00:00
LAL21447M	Laurence	A	Lebihan	5	175	0736	03-JUN-1990 00:00:00
ENL44273F	Elizabeth	N	Lincoln	14	35	0877	24-JUL-1990 00:00:00
PCM98509F	Patricia	C	McKenna	11	150	9999	01-AUG-1989 00:00:00
R-M53550M	Roland		Mendel	11	150	0736	05-SEP-1991 00:00:00
RBM23061F	Rita	B	Miller	5	198	1622	09-OCT-1993 00:00:00
HAN90777M	Helvetius	A	Nagy	7	120	9999	19-MAR-1993 00:00:00
TP055093M	Timothy	P	O'Rourke	13	100	0736	19-JUN-1988 00:00:00
SK022412M	Sven	K	Ottlieb	5	150	1389	05-APR-1991 00:00:00
MAP77183M	Miguel	A	Paolino	11	112	1389	07-DEC-1992 00:00:00
PSP68661F	Paula	S	Parente	8	125	1389	19-JAN-1994 00:00:00
M-P91209M	Manuel		Pereira	8	101	9999	09-JAN-1989 00:00:00
MJP25939M	Maria	J	Pontes	5	246	1756	01-MAR-1989 00:00:00
M-R38834F	Martine		Rancú	9	75	0877	05-FEB-1992 00:00:00
DWR65030M	Diego	W	Roel	6	192	1389	16-DEC-1991 00:00:00
A-R89858F	Annette		Roulet	6	152	9999	21-FEB-1990 00:00:00
MMS49649F	Mary	M	Saveley	8	175	0736	29-JUN-1993 00:00:00
CGS88322F	carine	G	Schmitt	13	64	1389	07-JUL-1992 00:00:00
MAS70474F	Margaret	A	Smith	9	78	1389	29-SEP-1988 00:00:00
HAS54740M	Howard	A	Snyder	12	100	0736	19-NOV-1988 00:00:00
MFS52347M	MartÏn	F	Sommer	10	165	0736	13-APR-1990 00:00:00
GHT50241M	Gary	H	Thomas	9	170	0736	09-AUG-1988 00:00:00
DBT39435M	Daniel	B	Tonini	11	75	0877	01-JAN-1990 00:00:00

The TITLES Table

Structure:

NAME	TBNAME	TBCREATOR	COLNO	COLTYPE
TITLE_ID	TITLES	SYSADM	1	VARCHAR
TITLE	TITLES	SYSADM	2	VARCHAR
TYPE	TITLES	SYSADM	3	CHAR
PUB_ID	TITLES	SYSADM	4	CHAR
PRICE	TITLES	SYSADM	5	DECIMAL
ADVANCE	TITLES	SYSADM	6	DECIMAL
ROYALTY	TITLES	SYSADM	7	INTEGER
YTD_SALES	TITLES	SYSADM	8	INTEGER
NOTES	TITLES	SYSADM	9	VARCHAR
PUBDATE	TITLES	SYSADM	10	TIMESTMP

Contents:

TITLE_ID	TITLE	TYPE	PUB_ID	PRICE	ADVANCE
BU1032	The Busy Executive's Database Guide	business	1389	19.99	5000
BU1111	Cooking with Computers: Surreptitious Balance Sheets	business	1389	11.95	5000
BU2075	You Can Combat Computer Stress!	business	0736	2.99	10125
BU7832	Straight Talk About Computers	business	1389	19.99	5000
MC2222	Silicon Valley Gastronomic Treats	mod_cook	0877	19.99	0
MC3021	The Gourmet Microwave	mod_cook	0877	2.99	15000
MC3026	The Psychology of Computer Cooking	UNDECIDED	0877		
PC1035	But Is It User Friendly?	popular_comp	1389	22.95	7000

Structure and Contents of Table ■ 239

LENGTH	SCALE	NULLS
6	0	Y
80	0	N
12	0	N
4	0	Y
15	4	Y
15	4	Y
4	0	Y
4	0	Y
200	0	Y
10	0	N

ROYALTY	YTD_SALES	NOTES	PUBDATE
10	4095	An overview of available database systems with emphasis on common business applications. Illustrated.	12-JUN-1991 00:00:00
10	3876	Helpful hints on how to use your electronic resources to the best advantage.	09-JUN-1991 00:00:00
24	18722	The latest medical and psychological techniques for living with the electronic office. Easy-to-understand explanations.	30-JUN-1991 00:00:00
10	4095	Annotated analysis of what computers can do for you: a no-hype guide for the critical user.	22-JUN-1991 00:00:00
12	2032	Favorite recipes for quick, easy, and elegant meals.	09-JUN-1991 00:00:00
24	22246	Traditional French gourmet recipes adapted for modern microwave cooking.	18-JUN-1991 00:00:00
			07-JUN-1995 14:39:08
16	8780	A survey of software for the naive user, focusing on the 'friendliness' of each.	30-JUN-1991 00:00:00

Contents: (continued)

TITLE_ID	TITLE	TYPE	PUB_ID	PRICE	ADVANCE
PC8888	Secrets of Silicon Valley	popular_comp	1389	20	8000
PC9999	Net Etiquette	popular_comp	1389		
PS1372	Computer Phobic AND Non-Phobic Individuals: Behavior Variations	psychology	0877	21.59	7000
PS2091	Is Anger the Enemy?	psychology	0736	10.95	2275
PS2106	Life Without Fear	psychology	0736	7	6000
PS3333	Prolonged Data Deprivation: Four Case Studies	psychology	0736	19.99	2000
PS7777	Emotional Security: A New Algorithm	psychology	0736	7.99	4000
TC3218	Onions, Leeks, and Garlic: Cooking Secrets of the Mediterranean	trad_cook	0877	20.95	7000
TC4203	Fifty Years in Buckingham Palace Kitchens	trad_cook	0877	11.95	4000

ROYALTY	YTD_SALES	NOTES	PUBDATE	
10	4095	Muckraking reporting on the world's largest computer hardware and software manufacturers.	12-JUN-1994	00:00:00
		A must-read for computer conferencing.	07-JUN-1995	14:39:08
10	375	A must for the specialist, this book examines the difference between those who hate and fear computers and those who don't.	21-OCT-1991	00:00:00
12	2045	Carefully researched study of the effects of strong emotions on the body. Metabolic charts included.	15-JUN-1991	00:00:00
10	111	New exercise, meditation, and nutritional techniques that can reduce the shock of daily interactions. Popular audience. Sample menus included, exercise video available separately.	05-OCT-1991	00:00:00
10	4072	What happens when the data runs dry? Searching evaluations of information-shortage effects.	12-JUN-1991	00:00:00
10	3336	Protecting yourself and your loved ones from undue emotional stress in the modern world. Use of computer and nutritional aids emphasized.	12-JUN-1991	00:00:00
10	375	Profusely illustrated in color, this makes a wonderful gift book for a cuisine-oriented friend.	21-OCT-1991	00:00:00
14	15096	More anecdotes from the Queen's favorite cook describing life among English royalty. Recipes, techniques, tender vignettes.	12-JUN-1991	00:00:00

Appendix G
Answers to Review Questions

Chapter 1

1. The database resides in the server.
2. A table is a collection of related data. It is composed of rows, which represent the records, and columns, which represent the fields.
3. An index is a database component used to accelerate row access.
4. A view is a virtual table. It acts like a table but its columns are actually columns from other tables.
5. A role is a group of attributes that can be assigned to a user.
6. A stored procedure is a SQL program stored in the database.
7. A trigger is a kind of stored procedure that is automatically executed when an INSERT, DELETE, or UPDATE statement is used.

Chapter 2

1. Embedded SQL is a SQL program inserted in another language such as COBOL or BASIC. Interactive SQL is the use of SQL using special programs in which the user can execute individual statements.
2. There are three types of SQL commands: DDL statements, DML statements, and DCL Statements.

3. DDL statements are used to create database objects.
4. DML statements are used to manipulate database tables.
5. DCL statements are used to set database features regarding security.
6. Data types are the different kinds of data supported by the database.
7. The int type has no decimals.

Chapter 3

1. The SELECT command retrieves rows and columns of a table.
2. See page 24.
3. The asterisk (*) represents all columns of the table.
4. The ALL clause represents all rows of the table.
5. The WHERE clause filters the table rows that are returned.
6. The CREATE TABLE command creates a new table in the current or specified database.
7. The INSERT command inserts a new row in a given table.
8. The DELETE command removes a row from the table.
9. The UPDATE command allows for the adjustment of a value in a given column.
10. The DROP TABLE command removes a table from the database.

Chapter 4

1. An expression is a combination of identifiers, values, and operators that the database can evaluate to get a result.
2. An expression's components are operators and operands like constants, variables, and functions.
3. The six operators are arithmetic, character, comparison, logical, bitwise, and unary.
4. A predicate is an expression that evaluates to TRUE, FALSE, or UNKNOWN.
5. The NULL predicate determines whether or not a given expression is NULL.
6. The EXISTS predicate specifies a subquery to test for the existence of rows.

7. The IN predicate determines if a given value matches any value in a subquery or a list.
8. The LIKE predicate determines whether or not a given character string matches a specified pattern.

Chapter 5

1. SELECT emp_name AS Name, emp_code AS Code FROM Emp.
2. The operator used to concatenate two text strings is || (two vertical bars).
3. SELECT city , 'is the hometown of ' , au_fname FROM Authors.
4. SELECT title, code, price, ytd_sales, ytd_sales*.10 AS royalties FROM Titles.
5. A table alias can make a SELECT command more understandable and also avoids conflicts between columns in different tables that have the same name.

Chapter 6

1. A function is a routine that performs a specific operation and returns a value.
2. The types of functions are row, aggregate, and scalar.
3. Aggregate functions operate on a collection of values but return a single, summarizing value.
4. The DISTINCT keyword eliminates duplicate rows from the results of a SELECT statement.
5. SELECT COUNT (price) FROM titles WHERE type='job'.
6. SELECT AVG (price) FROM titles WHERE type='job'.

Chapter 7

1. The ORDER BY clause specifies the sort for the result set.
2. The results of the ORDER BY clause are shown in ascending order by default.
3. To show the results of an ORDER BY clause in descending order, add the DESC clause.

4. To order results by two or more columns, specify the columns' names separated by commas.

5. The order in which the columns will appear is their order in the list.

Chapter 8

1. The GROUP BY clause creates subsets of summary information by organizing data into groups.

2. If the grouping column contains a null value, that row becomes a group in the results. If the grouping column contains more than one null value, the null values are put into a single group. This behavior is defined in the SQL-92 standard.

3. The HAVING clause sets conditions on the GROUP BY clause similar to the way WHERE interacts with SELECT. The WHERE search condition is applied before the grouping operation occurs; the HAVING search condition is applied after the grouping operation occurs. The HAVING syntax is similar to the WHERE syntax, except HAVING can contain aggregate functions. HAVING clauses can reference any of the items that appear in the select list.

4. To order a result set, add the ORDER BY clause.

Chapter 9

1. Join tables are tables that have had a relationship created between them by using common values.

2. An equi-join is a join created using a comparison operator based on equality.

3. The UNION clause combines the results of two or more queries into a single result set consisting of all the rows belonging to all queries in the union.

4. SELECT * FROM Table1
   UNION
   SELECT * FROM Table2
   UNION
   SELECT * FROM Table3

Chapter 10

1. A subquery is a SELECT query that returns a single value and is nested inside a SELECT, INSERT, UPDATE, or DELETE statement, or inside another subquery.

2. A correlated query is a subquery that references a column in the outer statement. The inner query is executed for each candidate row in the outer statement.

3. A non-correlated query is a subquery independent of the previous query.

4. When a subquery is introduced with the keyword EXISTS, it functions as an existence test. The WHERE clause of the outer query tests for the existence of rows returned by the subquery. The subquery does not actually produce any data; it returns a value of TRUE or FALSE.

5. The result of a subquery introduced with IN (or with NOT IN) is a list of zero or more values. After the subquery returns results, the outer query makes use of them.

6. The ALL modifier returns the greater value returned by the subquery.

7. The ANY modifier returns the smallest value of the rows returned by the subquery.

Chapter 11

1. Constraints are a mechanism used by the database to define rules regarding the values allowed in columns. They are the standard mechanism for enforcing integrity.

2. The CHECK constraint enforces domain integrity by limiting the values that can be placed in a column.

3. The UNIQUE constraint enforces the uniqueness of the values in a set of columns.

4. NOT NULL specifies that the column does not accept NULL values.

5. Primary key constraints identify the column or set of columns whose values uniquely identify a row in a table.

6. Foreign key constraints identify the relationships between tables.

7. Referential integrity indicates that the relationships between tables have been properly maintained. Data in one table should only point to existing rows in another table; it should not point to rows that do not exist.

8. An index allows the database program to find data in a table without scanning the entire table, thus reducing access time.
9. The CREATE TABLE command is used to create a table.
10. The DROP TABLE command is used to delete a table.

Chapter 12

1. The INSERT command inserts new rows in a given table.
2. See page 134.
3. The DELETE command removes rows of a given table.
4. See page 140.
5. The UPDATE command is used to change the contents of a column or group of columns.
6. See page 143.
7. The ALTER TABLE command can be used to change some of the characteristics of a table.

Chapter 13

1. A view can be thought of as either a virtual table or a stored query. The data accessible through a view is not stored in the database as a distinct object. What is stored in the database is a SELECT statement. The result set of the SELECT statement forms the virtual table returned by the view.
2. The CREATE VIEW command is used to create a view. See page 149 for the syntax.
3. The DROP VIEW command is used to delete a view. See page 153 for the syntax.
4. The data in the original table referenced by a view can be changed when the view uses data from a single table.
5. The CHECK OPTION clause restricts the types of updates that can be made in a table.

Chapter 14

No review questions

Chapter 15

1. Synonyms are alternate names for some database objects.
2. Public synonyms are synonyms visible to all database users.
3. See page 167 for the CREATE SYNONYM command syntax.
4. The CREATE USER command is used to create a user. See page 168 for the syntax.
5. The DROP USER command is used to delete a user. See page 170 for the syntax.
6. Privileges are the authorizations given to a user to access and manipulate database objects.
7. The GRANT command is used to create privileges. See page 173 for the syntax.
8. Roles allow you to collect users into a single unit to which you can apply permissions. Permissions granted to, denied to, or revoked from a role apply to all users with that role.
9. CREATE ROLE is used to create roles and DROP ROLE is used to delete roles.

Index

A
aggregate functions, 58, 59-62, 100
    restrictions, 63-64
aliases, creating, 51-52
ALL, 59, 109-11
ALTER TABLE, 144-146
ANY, 109-111
architecture,
    client/server, 4
    database, 5-7
arithmetic operators, 38
AS, 48
AVG, 59

B
BEGIN TRANSACTION, 181-182
BETWEEN, 41
bitwise operators, 39

C
calculated columns, 50-51
candidate key, 118
character operators, 39
CHECK OPTION, 155-156
client, 4
client/server architecture, 4
column names, 151-152
    alternate, 48
columns,
    calculated, 50-51
    concatenating, 49
    inserting information into, 135-140
    ordering, 68-69
    renaming, 48
    selecting, 26, 28
commands, 201-209
COMMIT, 182-183
comparison operators, 39

compound index, 128
constraints, 117-118
correlated queries, 99
COUNT, 59, 61-62
CREATE INDEX, 129-130
CREATE ROLE, 178
CREATE SYNONYM, 167
CREATE TABLE, 30-31, 119-124
CREATE USER, 168-169
CREATE VIEW, 149-151

D
data,
    grouping, 74-81
    updating, 154-155
data control language, 17
data definition language, 16, 22
data manipulation language, 16-17, 22-23
data types, 17-18
    Oracle 8, 215-217
    SQl Server 7, 213-215
    SQLBase, 23-24, 116-117, 217-218
database, 5-6
    architecture, 5-7
    objects, 7-12
    Oracle, 6
    SQL Server 7, 6-7
DCL, *see* data control language
DDL, *see* data definition language
DELETE, 32-33, 140
DESC, 67
DISTINCT, 59, 62-63
DML, *see* data manipulation language
DROP INDEX, 130
DROP ROLE, 179-180
DROP TABLE, 34-35, 127
DROP USER, 169-170
DROP VIEW, 153

Index

E
embedded SQL, 15, 158
equi-join, 87-88
error handling, 26-27
EXISTS, 43, 103-105
expressions, 38
    ordering by, 70
    using with tables, 139

F
fields, updating, 33-34, 143-144
filtering, 77-79
foreign key, 118-119, 141-143
functions, 58
    SQL, 185-199
    types of, 58

G
GRANT, 173-174, 178
GROUP BY, 74-76
group functions, *see* aggregate functions

H
HAVING, 78-79

I
IN, 45, 101-103
indexes, 10, 127
    compound, 128
    creating, 129
    removing, 130
INSERT, 31-32, 134-135
interactive SQL, 15

J
joining, 84
joins, 84-87, 90-92

L
LIKE, 44
local database, 6
logical operators, 39

M
MAX, 59-60
MIN, 60

N
nested subquery, 105-108
non-correlated queries, 98-99
NOT EXISTS, 104-105
NOT IN, 101-103
NULL, 42
null value, 40, 77-78, 118

O
object privileges, 172-173
operator precedence, 40
operators, 38-39
Oracle 8,
    data types, 215-217
    synonyms, 216-217
Oracle database, 6
ordering,
    by multiple columns, 168-169
    using column headers, 71
    using expressions, 70
ORDER BY, 66-67
    restrictions, 68
    using, 80-81

P
parameters, 11
parent key, 124
precedence, 40
predicates, 40
    BETWEEN, 41
    EXISTS, 43
    IN, 45
    LIKE, 44
    NULL, 42
    relational, 41
primary key, 118
privileges, 170-173
    granting, 173-174
    revoking, 174-177
procedural language, 14

Q
queries,
    combining, 28-29
    correlated, 99

Index

filtering, 29-30
non-correlated, 98-99

R

records, filtering, 77-79
referential integrity, 124-126
relational predicates, 41
results, ordering, 66-72
REVOKE, 174-177
roles, 9, 177-178
    creating, 178
    deleting, 179-180
    granting, 173-174, 178
    viewing, 179
ROLLBACK, 182
rows,
    deleting, 141-143
    inserting, 31-32, 134-139
    removing, 32-33

S

scalar functions, 58
SELECT, 24-30
server, 4
single row functions, see scalar functions
snapshots, 8
SOME, 109-111
SQL, 14
    characteristics, 14-16
    commands, 201-209
    data types, 211-218
    embedded, 15, 158
    functions, 185-199
    interactive, 15-16
SQL Server 7 database, 6-7
    data types, 213-215
    synonyms, 214-215
SQLBase,
    application, 158-163
    data types, 23-24, 116-117, 217-218
statement language, 15
stored procedures, 11
structured query language, see SQL

subquery, 98
    creating, 98-111
    nested, 105-108
    restrictions, 100
    return values, 99-100
SUM, 60
synonyms, 8, 166
    creating, 167
    Oracle 8, 216-217
    SQL Server 7, 214-215
system privileges, 170-172

T

tables, 7-8
    creating, 30-31, 119-124
    creating aliases for, 51-52
    defining, 116-119
    joining, 84-95
    modifying, 144-146
    removing, 34-35, 127
transactions, 180-181
    committing, 182-183
    initiating, 181-182
    rolling back, 182
triggers, 12

U

unary operators, 39
UNION, 28-29, 93-95
UNIQUE, 130
UPDATE, 33-34, 143-144
users, 8-9
    creating, 168-169
    deleting, 169-170

V

views, 11, 148-149
    changing date with, 154-155
    creating, 149-151
    deleting, 153
    querying, 153

W

WHERE, 29-30, 63-64, 77

ibooks.com offers you the best selection of online IT reference books

A full-service e-book source that gives you:
- browsing capability
- full-text searching
- "try-before-you-buy" previews
- customizable personal library
- wide selection of free books

www.ibooks.com

ADVANTAGE™
DATABASE SERVER
by Extended Systems

Looking for a high-performance SQL database solution that produces great results without adding complexity or ongoing maintenance costs?

Advantage allows you to develop and deploy applications FREE with Advantage Local Server. As you move to client/server, few code changes are necessary. Native tools allow you to develop applications with reduced time to market. And your final applications will be easy to install and deploy.

Stability, Performance and Scalability.

- Native SQL on both the remote and local server.
- High performance embedded client/server database solution.
- Eliminates database corruption.
- Scalable from local to peer-to-peer to client/server and Internet environments – with one set of source code.
- Supports simultaneous multi-user index and data access by means of an intelligent lock management system.
- Low maintenance – No DBA required.
- Royalty-free distribution for local and shared environments.

For more information call
800-235-7576 ext. 5030

or visit

www.AdvantageDatabase.com

Isn't it time for SQL to be faster, easier, and less expensive?

If you're looking for an exceptional client/server solution, this is the perfect opportunity. The enclosed CD contains the following software evaluations:

- **Advantage Database Server NT and NLM** (2-user versions)
- **Advantage Data Architect**
- **Free Clients with unlimited local server:**
  TDataSet Descendant for Delphi/C++Builder with source code to the VCL
  OLE DB Provider
  ODBC Driver
  Advantage Client Engine API
  Crystal Reports Driver
  Advantage Internet Server

FREE unlimited Web site access to FAQs and Advantage Knowledge Base

www.AdvantageDatabase.com

"We evaluated many different database options before selecting Advantage. No other product matched its speed, stability and price-point. Advantage surpassed our original expectations and the technical service is unparalleled in the industry. Advantage has been an integral partner in helping our customers, such as Best Buy, General Mills and UPS, automate their PR Departments."

Jason Siegal
Senior V.P., Sales and Product Development
Public Affairs Technologies, Inc.

"Not only is Advantage faster and more cost effective than InterBase®, Microsoft® SQL Server and Sybase® Adaptive Server (SQL Anywhere), they also provide better services and support. We continue to enjoy majority market share by providing leading technology and responsive customer care. Advantage does the same. Their support is excellent. I give it five stars."

David Cluff
Research & Development Director
MediSoft, Inc.

I don't have time for learning curves.

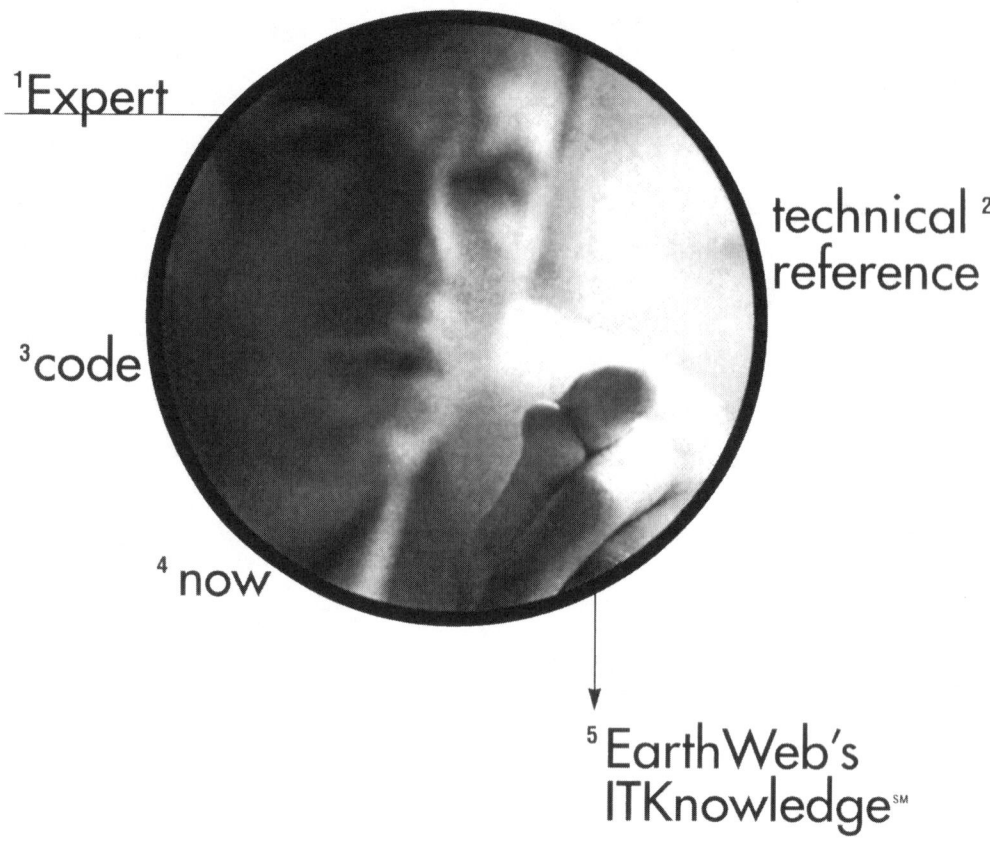

[1]Expert

technical[2] reference

[3]code

[4]now

[5]EarthWeb's ITKnowledge℠

They rely on you to be the ❶ expert on tough development challenges. There's no time for learning curves, so you go online for ❷ technical references from the experts who wrote the books. Find answers fast simply by clicking on our search engine. Access hundreds of online books, tutorials and even source ❸ code samples ❹ now. Go to ❺ EarthWeb's ITKnowledge, get immediate answers, and get down to it.

Get your FREE ITKnowledge trial subscription today at itkgo.com.
Use code number 026.

©1999 EarthWeb Inc. All rights reserved. EarthWeb's ITKnowledge is a service mark of EarthWeb, Inc. EarthWeb and the EarthWeb logo are registered trademarks of EarthWeb Inc.

EARTHWEB
Go further *faster*

The Companion CD

The companion CD-ROM contains a 60-day trial version of Centura Software Corporation's SQLBase database and an evaluation copy of Extended Systems' Advantage Database Server 5.7, in addition to an example database and a SQLBase application.

To install SQLBase, see Appendix D. To install the Pubssqlb database used in the examples, see Appendix E.

To install Advantage Database Server, open the Advantage folder, double-click on install.exe, and follow the on-screen instructions. For more information about this product, see the pages near the end of the book.

Be sure to change the read-only attribute of the working files to off.

Warning 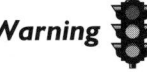 Opening the CD package makes this book nonreturnable.

CD/Source Code Usage License Agreement

Please read the following CD/Source Code usage license agreement before opening the CD and using the contents therein:

1. By opening the accompanying software package, you are indicating that you have read and agree to be bound by all terms and conditions of this CD/Source Code usage license agreement.

2. The compilation of code and utilities contained on the CD and in the book are copyrighted and protected by both U.S. copyright law and international copyright treaties, and is owned by Wordware Publishing, Inc. Individual source code, example programs, help files, freeware, shareware, utilities, and evaluation packages, including their copyrights, are owned by the respective authors.

3. No part of the enclosed CD or this book, including all source code, help files, shareware, freeware, utilities, example programs, or evaluation programs, may be made available on a public forum (such as a World Wide Web page, FTP site, bulletin board, or Internet news group) without the express written permission of Wordware Publishing, Inc. or the author of the respective source code, help files, shareware, freeware, utilities, example programs, or evaluation programs.

4. You may not decompile, reverse engineer, disassemble, create a derivative work, or otherwise use the enclosed programs, help files, freeware, shareware, utilities, or evaluation programs except as stated in this agreement.

5. The software, contained on the CD and/or as source code in this book, is sold without warranty of any kind. Wordware Publishing, Inc. and the authors specifically disclaim all other warranties, express or implied, including but not limited to implied warranties of merchantability and fitness for a particular purpose with respect to defects in the disk, the program, source code, sample files, help files, freeware, shareware, utilities, and evaluation programs contained therein, and/or the techniques described in the book and implemented in the example programs. In no event shall Wordware Publishing, Inc., its dealers, its distributors, or the authors be liable or held responsible for any loss of profit or any other alleged or actual private or commercial damage, including but not limited to special, incidental, consequential, or other damages.

6. One (1) copy of the CD or any source code therein may be created for backup purposes. The CD and all accompanying source code, sample files, help files, freeware, shareware, utilities, and evaluation programs may be copied to your hard drive. With the exception of freeware and shareware programs, at no time can any part of the contents of this CD reside on more than one computer at one time. The contents of the CD can be copied to another computer, as long as the contents of the CD contained on the original computer are deleted.

7. You may not include any part of the CD contents, including all source code, example programs, shareware, freeware, help files, utilities, or evaluation programs in any compilation of source code, utilities, help files, example programs, freeware, shareware, or evaluation programs on any media, including but not limited to CD, disk, or Internet distribution, without the express written permission of Wordware Publishing, Inc. or the owner of the individual source code, utilities, help files, example programs, freeware, shareware, or evaluation programs.

8. You may use the source code, techniques, and example programs in your own commercial or private applications unless otherwise noted by additional usage agreements as found on the CD.